HOW TO
CUT YOUR ENERGY BILLS

HOW TO
CUT YOUR ENERGY BILLS

Ronald Derven
Carol Nichols

Structures Publishing Company 1976
Farmington, Michigan   48024

Manufactured in the United States of America

Edited by Shirley M. Horowitz

Designed by Patrick Mullaly

Current Printing (last digit)
10 9 8 7 6 5 4 3 2 1

Library of Congress Cataloging in Publication Data

Derven, Ronald.
    How to cut your energy bills.

    Includes index.
    1. Energy conservation.   2. Dwellings—
Energy consumption.   I. Nichols, Carol, joint
author.   II. Title.
TJ163.3.D47   644   76-28727
ISBN 0-912336-28-5
ISBN 0-912336-29-3 pbk.

TABLE OF CONTENTS

Introduction

Until a few years ago, serious efforts to cut home energy consumption and waste were pursued by only a few builders, architects and homeowners. Energy was cheap, plentiful, and resources seemed virtually infinite. But the sudden, long dreary lines at gas stations a few years ago left a deep impression on a distressed public scrambling for gasoline. Now, greatly inflated home fuel bills are a painfully constant reminder that the world's fuel supplies are indeed limited!

Paying more for every type of fuel makes us aware that our disposable income is also finite and cannot be stretched to cover the inflationary spiral ahead of us. The increased costs of fuel have altered many people's life-styles. The Vermont homeowner who is now paying as much in energy costs as he or she does for the monthly mortgage payment (in some cases even more), has had to eliminate vacations altogether. The retired couple who moved to Florida on a fixed income for the good life is now seriously strapped to make ends meet. And middle-class working families are finding it difficult to maintain their standards of living.

Because few houses have been constructed with serious energy conservation in mind, there are innumerable ways to reduce your energy bills by 40 percent or more. A homeowner intent on retaining his or her disposable income to spend the way he or she desires can do so by reducing fuel bills to the level of a few years ago.

How to Cut Your Energy Bills is one of the few publications available today that can promise a return of more than the money invested in the price of the book. By reading and following its advice, hundreds of dollars can be saved each year.

This book is written expressly for people living in homes who want to reduce their energy bills immediately. It takes into consideration those who are contemplating the purchase of a new or older home, and is also written for the person contemplating building an addition or converting interior space (attic/basement/garage) into a room or rooms, desiring to maximize energy conservation from the start.

There is no one method of energy conservation, as the book details. There are several. But where does one begin? You can start anywhere in your home. But the main point is to close off *all* energy leaks. Then you should change the thinking of family members who might inadvertently be wasting or misusing energy and thereby adding to the monthly bill.

The book begins plugging the energy leaks at home with a chapter on insulation. This is a key area and no homeowner can hope to substantially reduce fuel use without a careful and complete study of insulation in the home. The chapter describes the virtues of every type of insulation: it tells how to apply insulation to finished attics, basement walls, hard-to-get-at crawl spaces and others; it also tells how to check a so-called "insulated" house to ensure the maximum amount. If you live in a cold area, for instance, and snow melts as soon as it touches the roof, you have a serious energy leak that may be costing you the price of a new camera or a weekend vacation each year.

Doors and windows come next. Stand in front of an exterior door in your home. If you can see the light of day on top, at the sides, or at the bottom of the door, you are literally throwing away $5 a year. Multiply this by how many doors you have. For pennies in materials and half an hour's work, the condition could be eliminated. As for windows, that view you like so much could be costing you a small fortune if the glass is not double-glazed or if storm windows are not added in the winter. Even if you do not want the expense of changing single-pane windows to double-glazed or the addition of aluminum storm windows, this book will show you two methods of producing storm windows for a fraction of the cost. The book also shows you why adding an inexpensive vestibule can cut heating loss through doors; details on weather stripping, caulking and many other items are also included.

The heating and air conditioning chapter will tell you how all popular systems work and how you can keep them in top condition to cut energy waste, and "tune up" most air conditioning systems for greater efficiency. Included are details on how to most effectively use humidifiers and dehumidifiers to save energy. Heat pumps offer a great deal of potential savings for old and new homes and they are discussed fully. Hot water heaters, a big piece of the yearly heating bill, are reviewed with several tried-and-true recommendations for saving energy.

Other in-depth topics in the book are: how to ventilate your house (which saves a great deal on air-conditioning and heating costs); lighting and appliances and how to maximize their use; fireplaces, alternative heat sources, how to take advantage of the sun's heat, and how to get a tax refund for installing insulation.

Some additional key chapters are energy conservation in home additions and conversion of interior space, and energy conservation for homes already built, with planning tips on building your own. Except perhaps for the very rich, virtually everyone must consider energy conservation during construction; this is covered from planning stages as to the best spot for a room addition or window placement on a converted garage, to the laying of a foundation or slab, on up to the shingles on the roof. For building a new home or adding on to an existing structure energy conservation features are crucial, but proper site planning is just as important. Proper placement of windows, trees, garage, etc., can save great amounts of energy.

Finally, no matter how well designed a house or addition or converted space is, anything less than 100 percent quality control during construction will result in loss of energy, and loss of money. Insulation, for instance, that is several inches thicker than in any other house in the area, is of no avail unless attached properly. These chapters will tell you how to check for quality control.

Buying a new house or an older unit? Checklists on buying an existing home will help you uncover any hidden energy leaks. It is a "must" today to check last year's energy bill with the seller. Chances are, the unit could be so poorly built that he or she is trying to sell it to get away from the high energy costs.

Another chapter gives all current details on future energy sources, many of which can be applied today. Finally, the book details some of the major energy-conservation homes now in existence. This chapter could offer you many valuable tips on achieving lower energy bills in your existing home, or for a home you are about to build.

An entire chapter is devoted to fitting your house for seasonal change and proper home energy management. Seasonal-change advice may mean that a few hours work on a weekend can save you money during the heating and cooling seasons; energy management can have an immediate effect on the monthly bill. Many tips included are just common sense, many are new and innovative. Wise energy management is as important as plugging up the leaks in the home. That is, if family X and family Y live next to each other in identical homes, family Y could use as much as 50 percent more energy a year than family X, just through sloppy management. The house that is over-heated all day and night in the winter or overcooled in the summer can boost the energy bill by 15 to 20 percent. Doors and windows left open, appliances misused, heating systems running inefficiently, lights left burning for no particular reason, can actually add many hundreds of dollars a year to the already high fuel bill.

On the other hand, good energy management without plugging the vast energy leaks in the home is an exercise in futility. The homeowner in a poorly insulated home can keep the thermostat low. He will achieve a lower energy bill but a great deal of discomfort as well.

The aim of this book, therefore, is threefold: to save the reader a great deal of money on energy costs, to allow him to live comfortably, and to hopefully ease some of the pressure on the world's fossil fuel supply.

1. Weather Barriers

THE KEY SAVER

Insulation is a key ingredient to big energy and dollar savings in the home. If no insulation now acts as a weather barrier in the unit, then the addition of even a little will dramatically reduce fuel bills. In homes which contain some, the addition of more insulation will result in a substantial savings.

In all likelihood the house you live in or are about to buy needs more insulation. If you spot a house during snow season and the roof is clean, beware of those heating bills. The insulation is not effective: heat is rising right through the attic roof and melting the snow. One study puts the number of houses with adequate insulation at one in ten. Another estimates that almost two-thirds of U.S. homes do not have enough insulation while another one-third has no insulation at all. The National Bureau of Standards (NBS) reported that 40 percent of the energy (and dollars) consumed in home heating and cooling are wasted. Inadequate insulation is the major culprit. Most homes, even today, lack sufficient insulation because energy conservation has never been a top priority for the government, the building industry, or the homeowner.

Before 1940 no insulation was required by major building codes. Until recently, the Minimum Property Standards (MPS) of the Federal Housing Administration (FHA) required only 1½ inches of insulation in the attic, the most important area in the home for insulation.

Federal codes have been updated so that today 6 inches of attic insulation are required. An estimate by the NBS indicated that by investing in those 6 inches a person living in a relatively mild climate who has no attic insulation can get all of his or her money back in one heating season in saved energy bills. This, of course, is only a minimum. In extreme climates, 12 inches of attic insulation should be installed.

Investing in insulation pays for itself heating season after heating season. A homeowner who invests in the minimum 6 inches, spending between $100 and $200, will save about $100 to $200 the *first* year. But over the next ten heating seasons the savings will mount to between $1,000 and $2,000—the price of a grand vacation or the downpayment on a new car.

And this comes only from adding insulation in the attic. Greater savings can obviously be obtained from adding insulation to the walls and floor. For maximum dollar savings on heating and cooling bills, the entire roof, wall and floor area exposed to outside temperatures and weather conditions should be insulated. You should use weather barriers to protect your entire house. Just as an insulated jug is used to keep hot drinks hot, and cold drinks cold, so your house must reach for this type of efficiency.

There is a great deal of stress today to add insulation in accordance with the climate in which you live. To be on the safe side, add as much insulation as you can to your house. There is a good reason for this. Recent interviews with government energy officials and building industry research people reveal that home energy costs will rise between 10 percent and 12 percent a year, well into future years. This means that if you currently pay $800 a year for energy, in ten years you could be paying at least $1,600. Add inflation to this and you could well be paying $2,000 a year to heat and cool your home. Investment in adequate insulation today will reap rewards for years to come.

Energy awareness can result in secondary benefits as well: financial columnists and consumer groups are now urging people to check energy bills as standard operating procedure when buying a home. If your energy bills are outlandishly high, you may have to cut the price of the house. So plan ahead for the sake of your home's resale value.

TAX SAVINGS

Not only do you save on lower bills, but the federal government has added an extra incentive! Pending federal legislation provides the homeowner with a tax credit of 30 percent of the first $750 of insulation expenses, up to $225. This credit is not a "tax deductible expense" that you take off the short or long form—it is an amount that can be directly subtracted from the total tax amount you owe, at the bottom line. In effect, money in the bank!

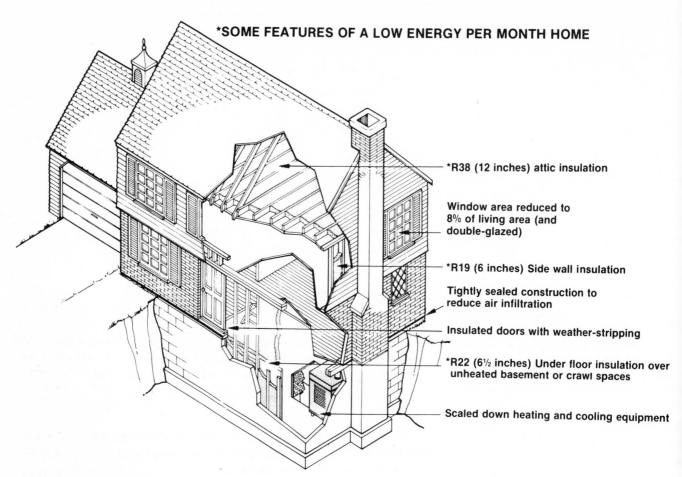

*SOME FEATURES OF A LOW ENERGY PER MONTH HOME

*R38 (12 inches) attic insulation

Window area reduced to 8% of living area (and double-glazed)

*R19 (6 inches) Side wall insulation

Tightly sealed construction to reduce air infiltration

Insulated doors with weather-stripping

*R22 (6½ inches) Under floor insulation over unheated basement or crawl spaces

Scaled down heating and cooling equipment

By protecting every area of your home from adverse weather conditions, you can cut your fuel bills to a minimum. Insulation is the prime ingredient for a "tight" house (Owens-Corning Fiberglas).

HOW INSULATION WORKS

All materials conduct at least some heat. Silver, copper and similar metals conduct heat rapidly and are, therefore, classified as "heat conductors." Wood and other fibrous materials conduct heat more slowly and are considered "heat insulators." Materials used in building insulation are of course heat insulators, but they have other characteristics as well: they are fireproof, verminproof and moisture-resistant.

The very best insulator we have available is air. Building insulation uses "trapped air" to achieve an effective heat barrier. In standard building insulation, air is trapped between millions of tiny fibers packed to a proper density. Proper density is the key: material packed too loosely will allow air to circulate and be dissipated by convection (convection is the transfer of heat through fluids). Material packed too tightly will allow heat loss by conduction (conduction is the transfer of heat through solids).

Besides greater energy and dollar savings achieved by adequate insulation, the material works in other ways to keep all of us more comfortable. During the winter, an uninsulated wall facing onto the exterior can be between eight degrees and fifteen degrees cooler than an insulated wall. By placing your hand on such a wall you can actually feel the cold. Through radiation all warm bodies lose heat to cooler bodies. This means the occupants sitting in a room with uninsulated exterior walls will actually lose heat to these walls even though the room temperature is 70 degrees. This phenomenon is known as the "cold wall effect," and occupants will turn the thermostat higher to feel comfortable. People sitting in a room with insulated walls will feel more comfortable with the same thermostat setting of 70 degrees.

The opposite occurs in the summer. Even though you may have the air conditioner running full blast, occupants in a room with uninsulated walls will absorb heat from the walls and possibly turn the thermostat lower to feel comfortable.

Besides causing discomfort, juggling the thermostat up and down can greatly add to fuel bills. If you can keep your thermostat three degrees lower in winter and three degrees higher in summer, you can save at least 5 percent on your annual fuel bill.

Another function of insulation is to keep the entire room at about the same temperature. In an uninsulated room, heated air near a cold wall will cool off and move to the floor while hot air will rise to take its place. This continuous circulation of air causes drafts. A room with well-insulated walls will, obviously, have fewer drafts.

Insulation Placement

As mentioned above, insulation must be placed in every area of the home which is exposed to the exterior. All locations which will reduce heat loss in the winter will prevent heat gain in the summer as well. No insulation is needed between two rooms within the house so long as both are kept at about the same temperature. The only time insulation is needed between two interior walls is when one room is left unheated or is only heated infrequently.

Here are specific areas which require insulation.

- Exterior walls—all exterior walls; sometimes overlooked are walls between the living space and unheated garages or storage areas.
- Ceilings—facing on cold spaces above.
- Knee walls—when attic is finished as a living area.
- Around perimeter of slab—if house is slab-on-grade.
- Floors—facing on cold spaces such as over garages, crawl spaces or porches when house is cantilevered.
- Basement walls—when area is heated or used as living space. When basement is unheated, the floor over the basement should be insulated.

''R'' Value

To compare apples with apples, all insulation is given an ''R'' value or ''Resistance to Heat Flow'' value. All insulation commercially available will be marked with an ''R'' value. On a typical insulation package, you will either see an R-6, R-11, R-19 and so on. This R value is given for a certain thickness of material or the way in which it is used. The higher the R value, the better insulator it will be.

Never underestimate the real value of insulation. It is often heard that an 8-inch concrete block wall, typically found in basements, does not need insulation because the blocks are insulation enough. The fact is, it would take a wall four concrete blocks thick to provide the same weather barrier obtainable with just one inch of properly applied mineral wool insulation. A typical wall has about 3½ inches of mineral wool insulation; now calculate how many concrete blocks you would need to obtain that insulating value.

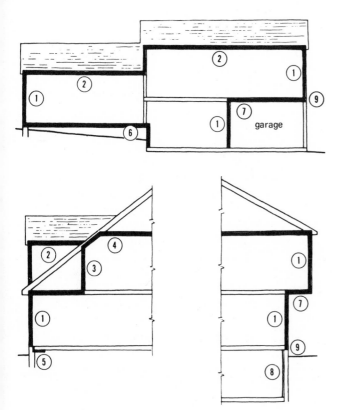

Specific areas which require insulation are: (1) exterior walls and walls between unheated and heated parts of the house; (2) ceilings with cold spaces above, and dormer ceilings; (3) knee walls when attic is finished; (4) between collar beams and rafters; (5) around perimeter of slab; (6) floors above vented crawl spaces; (7) floors above unheated or open spaces, garage or porch; (8) basement walls when space is finished; (9) in back of band or header joists (Mineral Wool Insulation Assn. Inc.).

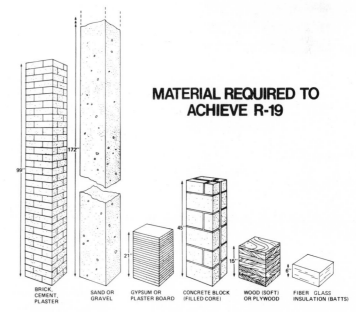

MATERIAL REQUIRED TO ACHIEVE R-19

Never underestimate the value of insulation. As shown above, a 6-inch layer of fiber glass insulation has the same insulation value (R-19) as more than 14 feet of sand or gravel (Certain-teed Products Corp.).

Buying Insulation

Today, typical insulation for the home is made from mineral fiber in batts or blankets, mineral fiber loose fills (these are either pneumatically installed by machine or spread by hand), cellulosic loose fills (machine-applied), foamed plastics (usually but not always in board form) and aluminum foil sheets.

Mineral Fiber. This has been on the market for a long time and is one of the oldest forms of modern insulation. Originally manufactured by melting down slag as a by-product of steel production, this material today is made of either rock wool or fiberglass. The materials are melted down and extruded as fibers. These fibers are joined together and with air trapped between fibers it makes an excellent and versatile insulating material.

Always use gloves and old clothes (which can be discarded later) when pushing and shoving this material into place. Some of the fibers break off and become airborne. For this reason, always wear a respirator when applying the material. A simple respirator can be obtained at local hardware outlets for under $3.

Cellulosic Fiber. Made from wood pulp. Although wood itself is not fire resistant, this material has been treated so that it is both fire and moisture resistant. Unlike mineral fiber, this insulation can be handled without injury to the skin but inhaling any type of insulation material should always be avoided.

Foamed Plastics. Includes substances such as polyurethane, polystyrene or urea formaldehyde. Some of these substances are used as packaging materials. For building insulation, they come in rigid boards which can be easily cut with a knife and put in place. These materials are usually more efficient per inch of thickness than fibrous insulation. Polystyrene for example has an R value of 4 per inch and polyurethane is 6 per inch. The materials are often used where space is at a premium such as in a refrigerator or freezer wall. Although fireproof, in a very hot fire these materials melt and give off a thick, toxic smoke. **These materials should never be used as a finished surface for a room in a living space. They must always be covered with at least ½ inch of gypsum wallboard to assure fire and smoke safety.**

Expanded Mineral Materials. These are loose fills usually blown or poured into place. Popular fills include both vermiculite and perlite.

Refer to the following table for various R values of different insulation, according to thickness.

What Insulation for Where

Insulation not only comes in a variety of materials, but these materials are used in different forms. Certain forms of insulation are more effective in certain areas of your home.

TYPE OF INSULATION

	BATTS OR BLANKETS		LOOSE FILL (POURED-IN)			
	glass fiber	rock wool	glass fiber	rock wool	cellulosic fiber	
R-11	3½"-4"	3"	5"	4"	3"	R-11
R-19	6"-6½"	5¼"	8"-9"	6"-7"	5"	R-19
R-22	6½"	6"	10"	7"-8"	6"	R-22
R-30	9½"-10½"*	9"*	13"-14"	10"-11"	8"	R-30
R-38	12"-13"*	10½"*	17"-18"	13"-14"	10"-11"	R-38

* two batts or blankets required.

Table gives various R-values for different thicknesses of insulation (Dept. of Housing & Urban Development).

Batts. These sheets are of matted glass fiber or rock fiber insulation, and are used in the floors of unfinished attics, unfinished attic rafters and the underside of floors. This insulation is best suited for standard joist or rafter spaces either 16 inches or 24 inches o.c. (on center). And it usually comes in sections 15 inches to 23 inches wide, 1 inch to 7 inches thick and 4 feet to 8 feet long. It is available with or without a vapor barrier (see section in this chapter on vapor barriers), depending on your needs. This material is relatively easy to handle because of its size, and excellent for areas where you can lay insulation in place. There is usually more waste in trimming batts to fit areas than with blankets.

Blankets. Available in glass fiber or rock wool, as above, and can be used in an unfinished attic floor, unfinished attic rafters, the undersides of floors, and in exterior walls. Standard rolls are 15 inches to 23 inches wide, 1 inch to 7 inches thick, and come in a variety of lengths. They come with or without vapor barriers. There is usually less waste with blankets than batts, but the material is more difficult to handle because the rolls are much longer than are batts.

Foamed in Place. Insulation is usually urea formaldehyde and can be used in unfinished attic floors and in finished frame walls. This form of insulation has a higher R value per inch thickness than the above-mentioned types, but it must be contractor-installed, and so is more expensive. A shoddy job is possible unless you hire a qualified contractor.

Rigid Board. Made of extruded polystyrene bead board, urethane board or fiberglass. Extruded polystyrene and urethane are vapor resistant, but bead board and glass fiber are not. All these materials come in thicknesses from ¾ inch to 4 inches and in widths from 24 inches to 48 inches. Materials can be used to insulate basement walls in existing homes. They have a high R value and are easy to install but must be covered with wall boards (because of the smoke danger). If you cannot install the wallboard yourself, hire a contractor—it will push the cost up, but installation of the wall boards is mandatory.

Loose Fill. Comes in several materials that include glass fiber, mineral wool, cellulosic fiber, vermiculite and perlite. Cellulosic fiber has about 30 percent more insulating value than rock wool for the same installed thickness, but may break down in a hot attic (see Chapter 4 to avoid a hot attic). You can pour it yourself on unfinished attic floors; it is especially suitable where joist spacing is irregular or where there are many obstructions. Loose fill can also be blown into finished walls and attics which have no insulation. This is an excellent choice for hard-to-get-to places. A reliable contractor must be used because if the spaces are not totally filled, you will not get the insulating value you desire.

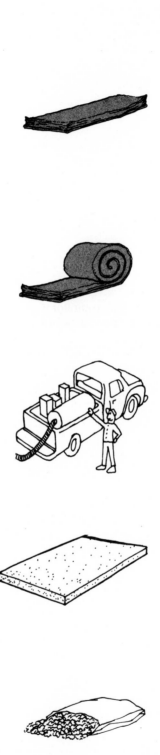

SUMMER COOLING ZONES

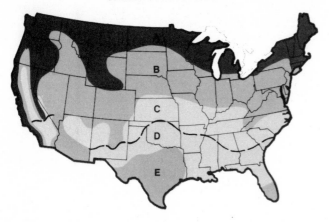

ATTIC INSULATION FOR SUMMER COOLING						
AIR CONDITIONING COST		RECOMMENDED INSULATION				
ELECTRIC (kWh)	GAS (therm)	ZONE A	ZONE B	ZONE C	ZONE D	ZONE E
1.5¢	9¢	—	—	—	R-11	R-11
2¢	12¢	—	—	R-11	R-11	R-11
2.5¢	15¢	—	—	R-11	R-11	R-19
3¢	18¢	—	R-11	R-11	R-11	R-19
4¢	24¢	—	R-11	R-11	R-19	R-30
5¢	30¢	—	R-11	R-19	R-19	R-30
6¢	36¢	—	R-11	R-19	R-30	R-30

WINTER HEATING ZONES

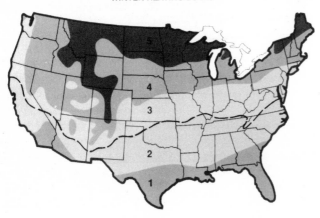

ATTIC INSULATION FOR WINTER HEATING								
HEATING COST				RECOMMENDED INSULATION				
GAS (therm)	OIL (gallon)	ELECTRIC RESISTANCE (kWh)	ELECTRIC HEAT PUMP (kWh)	ZONE 1	ZONE 2	ZONE 3	ZONE 4	ZONE 5
9¢	13¢	—	1¢	—	R-11	R-11	R-19	R-19
12¢	17¢	—	1.3¢	—	R-11	R-19	R-19	R-30
15¢	21¢	—	1.7¢	—	R-11	R-19	R-30	R-30
18¢	25¢	1¢	2¢	—	R-11	R-19	R-30	R-30
24¢	34¢	1.3¢	2.6¢	R-11	R-19	R-30	R-33	R-38
30¢	42¢	1.6¢	3.3¢	R-11	R-19	R-30	R-33	R-38
36¢	50¢	2¢	4¢	R-11	R-30	R-33	R-38	R-44
54¢	75¢	3¢	6¢	R-11	R-30	R-38	R-49	R-49
72¢	$1.00	4¢	8¢	R-19	R-38	R-44	R-49	R-60
90¢	$1.25	5¢	10¢	R-19	R-38	R-49	R-57	R-66

Find the amount of insulation you need on these weather maps and tables (Certain-teed Products Corp.).

How Much Insulation?

You can select the amount of insulation on the basis of climate, fuel cost, and type of heating system. The accompanying maps and tables can give you a rough estimate. In some parts of the country, where higher priced fuels are used, R-38 insulation in the attic is recommended for best results.

CHECKING YOUR HOME FOR PROPER INSULATION

Assume your house is guilty of inadequate insulation until proven otherwise. The first place to check is your attic.

Attics

They come in every shape and every stage of completion. Your attic may be completely finished, or it may be unfinished to the point where roof rafters are showing and no floor boards are in place. Regardless of the stage of completion, it must be insulated. But you must make a decision. If your attic is unfinished, and you plan to keep it that way, you can insulate between the floor joists. If, however, you intend to convert your attic to a living space (see chapter 8 for details), you should insulate the roof rafters and sidewalls and dormers (if you have them) instead. If you're not sure, opt to insulate the attic floor. This is a smaller area and will be less expensive and easier.

An unfinished attic, obviously, is the easiest place to check the insulation—either it's there or it's not; either there's enough or there's not enough. If "some" insulation is apparent, take a ruler and measure its thickness. Then look at the table on p. 12 to estimate the R-value of your attic insulation. If it is less than R-18, some additional insulation should be added.

In finished or semi-finished attics, the search may be a bit more difficult. There are two areas your insulation could be: either in roof rafter, end walls and dormers, *or* under the floor boards.

Finished or unfinished attics require insulation, although in different parts of the space (Dept. of Housing & Urban Development).

By measuring the depth of your attic insulation, you will be able to determine how much more you need to install to reach the proper R Value (Certain-teed Products Corp.).

In order to incorporate more insulation, 2 by 6 studs on 24-inch centers are used here instead of the more conventional 2 by 4 studs on 16-inch center system. This framing method enables 6 inches of insulation to be laid in the walls and because less lumber is used, the cost of additional insulation is partially offset (Owens-Corning Fiberglas Corp.).

If the attic is finished, insulation has been installed in the roof rafters, end walls and dormers. Usually in a finished attic, closets might be unfinished. This might be a good place to check the quality of insulation. If closets are finished, you will probably have to remove a portion of wall board or paneling to determine if insulation is behind it. If there are electrical outlets in the attic, you might be able to remove the switch plate and shine a flashlight in to determine the amount of insulation. (Always turn electrical power off before removing switch plate.) In any event, **the roof rafters, side walls and dormers must be checked separately.**

If upon investigation there is no insulation in those areas, then check under the floor board. The easiest way is to slip a ruler in between a crack in the floor boards and shine a flashlight in to determine the extent of insulation. The most accurate way to measure the insulation is to remove a floor board with a pry bar and measure carefully.

Walls

Most homes are constructed with wood frame walls. Here the siding and interior finish are attached to 2 x 4 inch support members called studs, which are either 16 inches or 24 inches o.c. This type of construction is used even in houses which have an exterior brick or stucco finish.

The simplest way to check wall insulation is to turn off the electrical power coming into the house, then remove the switch plate. Shine a flashlight into the space and see how much (if any) is there. Another way to check for adequate insulation if you're in the heating season, is to feel the inside of an exterior wall. If a wall is adequately insulated, it should be about room temperature. If not, it will feel cold to the touch. If your walls feel cold, don't

despair! Methods will be fully described in a following section for insulating these walls.

Electrical outlets themselves can be a problem with reference to wall insulation. The electrician who installed wiring in your house may have pulled the insulation away from the area where he installed the electrical fixture. This might cause a draft. A quick check of all switches and outlets in your house will pay off in lower heating or cooling bills. If it is a cold day you may be able to feel a distinct draft while standing in front of the outlet without even removing the switch plate! This is easily rectified by removing the plate and stuffing some fibrous insulation around the unit.

Basements and Underside of House

Regardless of the type of house you have, considerable money can be saved on fuel bills by insulating the underside of your house whether it has a full basement or crawl space.

In an unfinished basement it is easy to determine the amount of insulation. If the area is unfinished and bare masonry walls are showing, you have zero insulation. Now check the basement ceiling. If you don't see it, you don't have it. In a heated basement you definitely need insulation in the walls and not in the ceiling. (Remember, to gain the insulation qualities of 1 inch of mineral fiber insulation you would need a masonry wall 4 blocks thick.) In an unheated basement, you do not need insulation in the walls unless you intend to use the area as a living space. You must, however, insulate the ceiling to prevent heat loss.

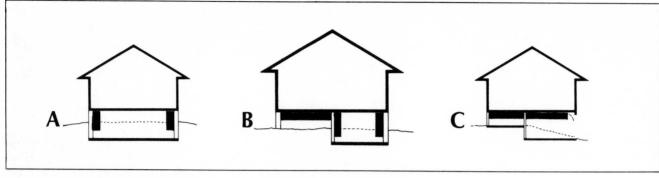

Insulating the underside of your house is necessary. (A) For heated basements the underside means the walls. (B) Combination of heated basement and unheated crawl space, the underside means the walls of the basement and top of crawl space. (C) Combination of unheated garage and unheated crawl space, underside means ceiling of garage and crawl space (Dept. of Housing & Urban Development).

If the basement is finished, make a careful check of walls to see that insulation is installed. Do this by removing a portion of the wall finish. Use the switch plate technique if you don't want to bother removing a piece of wall. In both finished and unfinished basements you should have at least 1 inch of rigid board insulation in walls *or* 3¾ inches of batt or blanket insulation in the ceiling.

Houses without basements will either have a crawl space (opened or closed) or slab-on-grade. Houses with an open crawl space will have insulation (if there is any) between floor joists directly above the space—either batt or blanket. Houses with a closed crawl space will have insulation either in the floor joists or on the sidewalls of the crawl space as in the accompanying illustration.

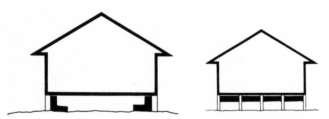

Two ways to insulate your crawl space (Dept. of Housing & Urban Development).

When checking the crawl space you should look for a minimum of 6 inches of insulation. If your house has less than that, add insulation following the directions in the next section of this chapter.

With homes built on a slab, it is impossible to tell if there is insulation under it. But one check you can make is the insulation around the footings. As a minimum, there should be rigid board insulation completely around the perimeter of the house at the footing going into the ground down to the frost line (usually 18 to 24 inches).

But sometimes this insulation is run vertically under the baseboard to the depth of the slab, and then horizontally under the slab for 24 inches or more.

Hot Water Pipes and Heating Ducts

Often ducts and pipes from your heating system pass through uninsulated areas of your home, such as an uninsulated crawl space. In this situation, the air or water you pay to heat is being dissipated before it enters the living space. To check this, follow the ducts from the furnace. If a duct or pipe passes through an uninsulated area, it should be insulated with material wrapped around it. The same is true for water pipes.

Duct insulation comes generally in blankets 1 or 2 inches thick. Get the thicker variety, particularly if you've got rectangular ducts. For air conditioning ducts make sure you get the kind of insulation that has a vapor barrier. Seal the joints of the insulation tightly with tape to avoid condensation.

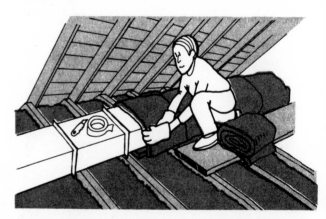

Heating ducts shown here, and hot water pipes which pass through uninsulated areas, should be wrapped with insulating material (Dept. of Housing & Urban Development).

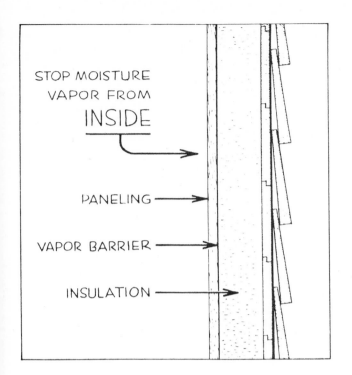

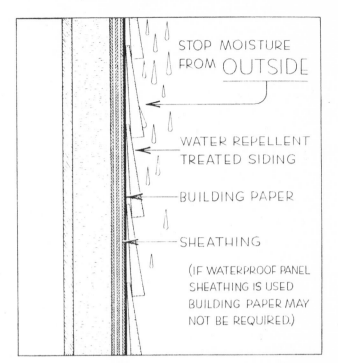

VAPOR BARRIERS

A key ingredient to proper insulation is to have sufficient vapor barriers. What is a vapor barrier? It is one of several types of materials which restrict the entry of water vapor into or through insulation where it could condense either in the insulation or on components of the wall framing such as wood studs, sheeting or siding. This can result in wet (and less effective) insulation, rotting structural member and sometimes peeling paint.

Blanket and batt type insulation come with a vapor barrier attached. The vapor barrier is always installed on the side where the heat is to be retained in winter. This type of insulation is stapled to wall or ceiling members. The staple can puncture the vapor barrier and so allow moisture to seep through. A sure cure for this is to cover the entire wall with 4 mil plastic.

Vapor barriers also help maintain a healthy level of humidity in rooms—from 30 to 40 percent.

HOW TO INSULATE THE ATTIC

Before putting any insulation in the attic, all water leaks must be sealed. Even if the weather is dry when you begin this task you can still discover water leaks. Portions of the roof board, rafters or perhaps the floor immediately adjacent to a water leak, will be discolored by the moisture. If the condition has persisted for a while, deterioration of the wood could be apparent.

In most cases the repair of the leak can be accomplished by replacing a few shingles. If numerous leaks are apparent, your entire roof might need replacing. Call in a qualified roofing specialist or repair the roof yourself *before* you begin insulating.

As mentioned previously, you must decide on future use of the attic. If the attic is unfinished and you intend to keep it that way, it is cheapest and easiest to insulate the floor. If you intend to finish off the attic into a living space, do not insulate the floor, rather insulate the roof rafters, side walls and dormers.

Unfinished

One of the easiest do-it-yourself tasks for a bill-conscious homeowner even if he or she is not especially handy around the house is to insulate the floor of an unfinished attic. To estimate the amount of insulation you will need multiply the length by the width. Then you must adjust this number to allow for the area taken up by floor joists. In your attic, your joists will be either 16 inches o.c. or 24 inches o.c. If 16 inches o.c., multiply length by width by .90 to arrive at the number of square feet you need. If 24 inches o.c., multiply length by width by .94 to total.

If you plan to use either blankets or batts, purchase insulation in the width you need plus length enough to satisfy the square footage. If you are going to use loose fill insulation, the bag will tell you the number of square feet it will cover to achieve a certain R-value.

Once you know the square footage of insulation needed, estimate the R-value you wish to achieve. For example, if you have 4 inches of mineral wool insulation in the attic floor, by checking the table on p..12 you will quickly see that you have a value of approximately R-12. If you wish to boost this to R-30, subtract R-12 from R-30, which equals R-18. Therefore you will need to add about 6 inches of mineral wool to achieve the value of R-30. It must be remembered, however, that to obtain the proper weather barrier, the insulation must be properly installed. Insulation rated at R-3 could act as a better barrier than poorly installed R-6 insulation.

Installing Vapor Barriers

Staple or tack polyethylene vapor barrier between joists. Seal seams and holes with tape (Dept. of Housing & Urban Development).

If both your existing insulation and the added insulation have vapor barriers, cut holes in the new insulation's vapor barrier (National Mineral Wool Insulation Assn. Inc.).

If no insulation is present in the attic floor, vapor barriers must be added. As can be seen in the illustration, a plastic vapor barrier must be stapled on the heated side of the insulation before the insulation is added, unless insulation incorporating a vapor barrier is used. If some insulation is present, a vapor barrier is also probably there, **do not add another.** Use batts or blankets or loose fill without a vapor barrier. If your insulation has a vapor barrier, cut holes in it as in the illustration. Failure to do so may cause an accumulation of moisture between the two layers of insulation.

The following illustrations detail the proper way to install insulation in the attic floor. You will need only a few tools to complete this task. These include a sharp knife, a straightedge ruler, measuring tape and a rake (to stuff insulation into tight corners and walk boards).

If the unfinished attic is partially finished with floor boards in place, insulation can be completed by removing several floor boards and stuffing insulation under others.

This sequence illustrates the proper way to install insulation on the attic floor (see below). (1) Begin at eaves on one side and work between several rows of joists. (2) Push batts under eaves with long stick. Do not butt insulation tightly against eaves because ventilation there is necessary. (3) Pressing batts down firmly, work toward center of the attic. (4) Use same procedure on opposite end of attic working from eaves to center. (5) When you come to center of attic, cut insulation to fit, saving leftovers for unfinished rows. (6) Start new rows until job is complete. (7) Cut insulation to fit around obstacles. Do not cover vents, recessed lighting fixtures, or exhaust fan motors protruding into attic (Certain-teed Products Corp.).

(1)

(2)

(3)

(4)

(5)

(6)

(7)

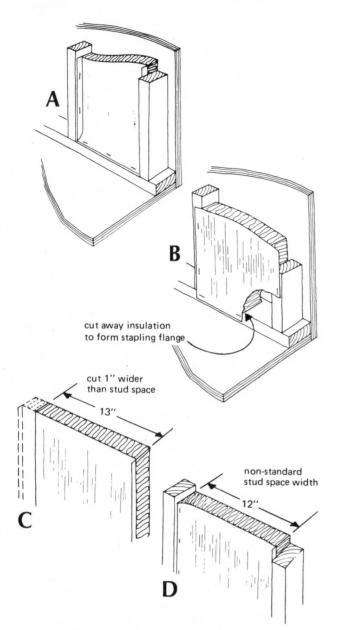

Working from the top on down, space staples 8 inches apart, fitting flanges tightly against sides (A) or faces (B) of studs. Insulate non-standard width spaces by cutting the insulation and the vapor barrier an inch or so wider than the space to be filled (C). Staple uncut flange as usual. Pull the vapor barrier on the cut side to the other stud, compressing the insulation behind it, and staple through vapor barrier (D) (National Mineral Wool Insulation Assn. Inc.).

If you plan to finish your attic and want to insulate for it, install insulation in the rafters and walls. Installing blankets or batts between roof rafters or end walls is accomplished in a similar manner to floors. Fit one end of the blanket or batt snugly against the top piece of the framing (as in the illustration) with the vapor barrier facing into the heated attic space. Working down, staple the flanges to the sides or the faces of the studs about 8 inches

apart (see illustration). Cut the blanket to fit tightly against the framing at the bottom (see illustration). If more than one piece of blanket or batt is used in the same stud space, butt the ends tightly together.

Because insulation comes in standard lengths to fit cavities either 16 inches or 24 inches o.c., it may be necessary to cut the insulation to fit it into a tighter or an

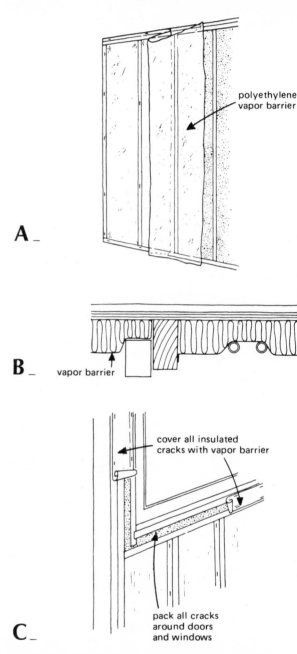

For highly effective vapor barrier, wedge pressure-fit blankets into space. Cover the inside face of the wall studs with polyethylene sheet (A). (B) Push insulation behind pipes, ducts and electrical boxes. (C) Pack small spaces between rough framing and door and window headers, jambs, and sills with pieces of insulation. Staple over with vapor barrier (National Mineral Wool Insulation Assn. Inc.).

irregular wall space. To do this, cut the insulation about 1 inch wider than the measured space. Staple the flange to one side of the stud wall, then pull the vapor barrier on the other side to its stud and staple, through the barrier.

These walls can also be insulated with unfaced insulation, in which case a separate vapor barrier must be added. Using either 2-mil or thicker polyethylene sheeting, press the material flat against the studs and staple about every 8 inches. Take care when handling material so that it is not punctured. If an accident does occur, tape the tear or puncture with electrical tape.

Insulating a finished attic is a bit more difficult. If you cannot get to the unfinished part of your attic without tearing up either the floors or walls, it might be best to call in an insulating contractor who can blow insulation into the required areas. He will drill relatively small holes in the wall and, using an air compressor, shoot loose fill insulation into the cavities. Although this will cost you considerably more than a do-it-yourself project, contractor-installed insulation will still eventually pay for itself in lower energy bills.

HOW TO INSULATE WALLS

Sidewalls of a house should be insulated to at least a value of R-11, which means between 3½ to 4 inches of blanket or batt mineral fiber or loose fill insulation. For new homes or additions, the blankets are probably easiest to install for the do-it-yourselfer. For older homes, the best option is to bring in a qualified insulating contractor and have him fill the walls with one of several loose fill materials.

In existing homes sidewalls can be insulated by a contractor who will blow in one of several loose fill materials (National Mineral Wool Insulation Assn. Inc.).

You must be very careful with contractor-installed insulation in walls and other cavities because once the material is in, you will not be able to really check the work. Before you sign a contract make sure that it is clearly understood what type of insulation you want in order to achieve a particular R-value. By looking at the table on Page 12 and reading the section on insulation types in this chapter, you can speak knowledgeably to any contractor.

If you select loose fills such as mineral fiber or cellulosic fiber, you can always check the bags to be sure of the R-value and to determine exactly how much insulation the contractor installs in your walls. If you opt for one of the foam insulations, there is really no way to check the quality. When obtaining an estimate for the job, contractors can usually estimate within 5 or 6 bags. If the contractor is a little over or under the figure he estimates, don't be surprised. There is nothing wrong with asking the contractor to save all empty bags for a final count.

The one problem with blowing loose fills into a wall is the vapor barrier. There is no way to blow a vapor barrier into a wall along with the insulation. Yet it is needed. To get around this, two coats of aluminum-in-varnish paint can be applied to the walls as an effective vapor barrier. Another method is to apply two or more coats of a good alkyd base semigloss paint over the primer coat of aluminum paint on walls. A good washable plastic wallpaper will also act as a substantial vapor barrier. If you have never wallpapered before, you might want to stick with paint; it's cheaper and simpler.

HOW TO INSULATE THE BASEMENT

If the basement is to remain an unheated space used for storage and little else, the cheapest and least time-consuming way to insulate is to do the ceiling of the basement. Use either blankets or batts at least 4 to 6 inches thick to achieve an R-value from 12 to 18. The easiest method is to face the vapor barrier up into the house and then place insulation between the joists and secure it by stapling wire mesh to the joists.

If the basement will be used for family entertainment or a home workshop, you must insulate the walls. Before beginning wall insulation, however, you must seal up all leaks. Moisture in the basement is often a tricky problem and can affect insulation. Sometimes it can be stopped by painting the lower portion of the foundation with a waterproofing paint. If the problem is serious, you may have to call in a water-diversion specialist.

For basement walls, use rigid boards or batts or blankets. Boards of 1 or 2 inches will give you adequate insulation or mineral fiber batts or blankets of 3 inches will

Install insulation in the floor joists of an unheated basement using either blankets or batts for an R-value of 12 to 18 (National Mineral Wool Insulation Assn. Inc.).

One area of potential heat loss occurs near the rim or band joist. A small piece of insulation above the furring and against the sill will insulate the band joist.

How to Insulate Crawl Space

If your home has a crawl space or is located over an unheated garage, insulate the joists as described in the previous section. Another method for insulating an enclosed crawl space is to lay insulation on the side of the enclosure and across the ground. Starting at the top of the crawl space wall, extend across the earthen area and up the other wall. A plastic vapor barrier should be carefully placed on the ground *before* work is begun. Unless you insulate the crawl space this way, it is important to have proper ventilation in the crawl space to keep moisture in check. For complete details see Chapter 4 on ventilation.

serve also. As can be seen in the following illustration you will need lumber for this operation. To support insulation in place, make a stud wall using 2 x 3 inch members either 16 inches or 24 inches o.c. Hammer a bottom plate to the floor and a top plate to the top of the masonry wall. Then insert 2 x 3s at your specified distance. The insulation can then be fitted between the 2 x 3s and stapled in place.

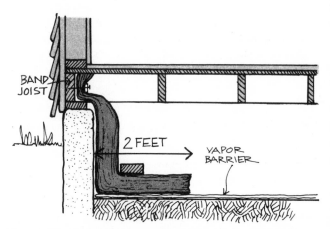

One method for insulating crawl spaces is to lay insulation on the side of the wall and across ground. Be sure to insulate band joist (Dept. of Housing & Urban Development).

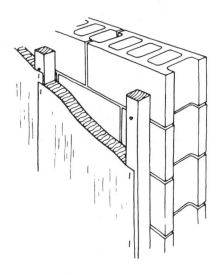

To insulate masonry wall, nail studs into place, fit insulation in between and put up vapor barrier (National Mineral Wool Insulation Assn. Inc.).

2. Windows and Doors

Saving your energy dollars means sealing energy leaks which occur in your home from your family's normal use of it. Although adding insulation (see Chapter 1) is the best way to start, the next place to look is at your doors and windows. And the best way to look at them is skeptically.

As a rule of thumb, if you stand inside your home and can see through to the outside, that spot is a dollar drain on your energy bill. It doesn't matter whether some of the "see-through" places are unintentionally planned, such as hair-line cracks, or if they were planned carefully and lovingly, such as windows and doors.

No window or door, no matter how well insulated and protected, can offer the same efficiency as a well-insulated wall. But you may very well be adding an unnecessary amount of money onto your bill if your doors and windows aren't "tight." You can estimate that between 30 percent to 50 percent of your total energy loss may be flying out your windows and doors.

CAUSES

As already mentioned, there is bound to be energy loss through your windows and doors—the trick is to keep it at an absolute minimum. The dollars are lost through the normal processes of (1) conduction, (2) radiation, and (3) air infiltration.

Conduction

Basically glass is a conductor of heat. When your house is warmer inside than out, the glass will conduct air from warmer to cooler. There go your heating dollars. It works in reverse during the hot months when warm air is conducted through your windows to heat up the cooler air in your house.

Radiation

Sun radiation in the winter is good for your heating bills, but it's a curse during the hot summer months. The sun's rays are radiated through the windows causing heat buildup at a tremendous rate. Radiation heat is a stealthy energy thief. It sneaks up during the day, and after sundown your cooling apparatus works double or tripletime to get rid of the heat buildup.

Air Infiltration

Air infiltration is a problem around windows and doors if they aren't properly sealed. This occurs when you can actually feel a draft coming from them when they're closed. After several years you can expect to feel that draft from windows and doors simply through normal everyday use. Starting from scratch, a high degree of energy efficiency can be achieved with windows and doors (Chapter 9 on new home additions tells you how), but this chapter deals with windows and doors already in existence in your home.

WINDOWS

Although you would assume that a home with large windows consumes more energy dollars than a house with smaller windows, this is not necessarily true. A house with spacious windows that are well designed, well located, and used properly can actually help save dollars on your energy bills. Poorly designed, poorly located windows that are used improperly can run up the monthly bill considerably.

Large windows located on the south of your home, with good exposure to the winter sun, can help heat your home with solar energy. That energy costs you absolutely

Spacious and well designed windows are not necessarily an energy burden. Here, double pane windows that act as outside mirrors located on the south, capture the rays of the winter sun to help heat the interior with solar energy (Libbey-Owens-Ford Co.).

POSITION OF SUN AT NOON FOR LATITUDE 40° NORTH

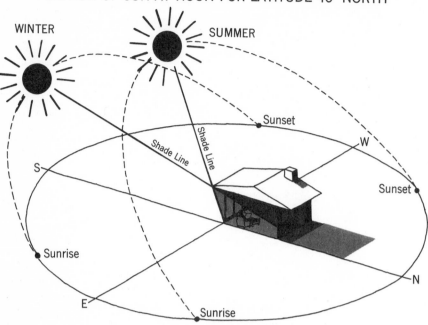

The seasonal elevation of the sun plus window exposures can influence your energy bills. The sun reaches windows placed on the south during the winter; it streams in windows facing east and west during the summer (Dept. of Agriculture).

nothing. Windows on the north side help you keep cool in the summer, but become energy thieves in freezing weather by stealing your heating dollars. Windows on the east or west side of the house cannot contribute much towards solar heat in the winter because of the southern angle of the sun. But in May, June and July when the sun reaches its northernmost boundaries, the sun will stream in east and west windows and cause considerable heat buildup. That's just about the time you turn on your air conditioner to keep cool.

Unfortunately you cannot only have your windows facing the south if you live in a cold climate, nor to the north if you live in a warm one. There are many ways to compensate for disadvantageous exposures from windows which otherwise offer good natural light, good air circulation, and a good view.

To make sure that the view you love so much isn't costing you a bundle of money: check the glass itself, note the exposure for your climate, and finally look closely at the installation of the window unit. You are actually checking, of course, for conduction, radiation, and air infiltration problems.

Conduction Problems

In a typical wood-frame house, a wall insulated with 3¾ inches fiberglass batts will have a value of R-15 (see chart in Chapter 1 on retardant values). A single pane of glass

(called a single-glazed window), about ⅛ inch thick, has an R-value of approximately 1. A single-glazed window will easily permit heat to escape to the cold outside, or conduct heat from the outside into the cool interior. Air, however, is an insulator—and luckily it's an insulation we can see through. To take advantage of this, we have double-glazed and triple-glazed windows.

Double-glazed windows are made up of double-insulated glass, usually with a ½ inch air space between the two panes. Glass with ¼ inch air space is also common—not as good, but cheaper. The ½ inch air space is more often found in commercial construction than in residential. The two panes of glass enclose a hermetically sealed space of dehydrated air. This acts as the insulation and has an R-value of about 1.5. Double-glazed windows are good; triple-glazed windows are even better. The three layers of glass enclose two separate air spaces and offer an R-value of about 2.9.

When it's zero (Fahrenheit) outside and 70 degrees inside your home, a single-glazed window will have a temperature on the inside surface of 18 degrees! This is 14 degrees below freezing right inside your home. The double-glazed window maintains a temperature of 36 degrees on the inside surface, while triple-glazed windows enable a surface temperature of 51 degrees.

Adding an extra layer of glass to a single-glazed window will keep the temperature near the floor 3 degrees warmer. In terms of energy consumption, going from

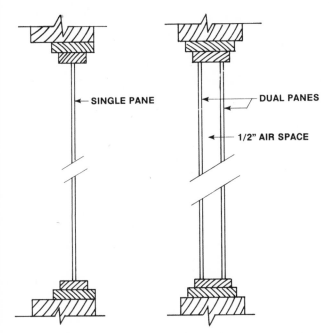

Using double-glazed windows instead of single-glazed can mean an energy loss reduction of 50 percent (Owens-Corning Fiberglas).

single-glaze to double-glaze means an energy loss reduction of 50 percent, from single-glaze to triple-glaze means a reduction of 65 percent. Going from double to triple will reduce the loss by only 15 percent.

Obviously a solution to the conduction problem is to add air insulation through double-glazed or triple-glazed windows. Hermetically sealed air spaces in "thermopane" windows is one way to provide the insulation; another way is adding an extra layer of glass with storm windows. After doing this (how to purchase or make your own storm windows is outlined further on in this chapter), you may want to consider buying or making thermal-lined drapes. These are effective against conduction and radiation because they act as both an insulator and light blocker. They also have an advantage in that you can close them at night during the winter and open them to receive the full amount of solar energy during the day. Keeping them drawn in the summer daylight hours could also save on your cooling bill.

Radiation Problems

Insulation through extra glazing or thermal drapes can help radiation problems, too. Because you are warmer than the window, your body radiates heat to that cold surface. You will, therefore, feel colder and more uncomfortable in a room with single-glazed windows and no thermal drapes than you will in a room with protected windows.

In warm climates where radiation can be a terrible problem, reflective double-glass windows are now available. They help keep out about 75 percent of the sun's radiation. Blinds, shades, curtains and shutters as well as thermal drapes can block out both the summer radiation problems and the simpler warm-weather heat conduction problem.

Two solutions to the radiation problem in hot weather: reflective glass which absorbs heat (Libbey-Owens-Ford Co.), and decorative shades (Window Shade Mfgrs. Assoc.).

Air Infiltration

Air infiltration is the unregulated entry of air into the living space of your home. This is quite different from ventilation (see Chapter 4) which is the necessary, controlled entry of air. Air infiltration is a serious problem in most homes because of natural wear and tear or faulty installation, so that a certain amount of heated air in the summer or frigid air in the winter is usually seeping in through the window units.

As previously stated if you can stand by one of your windows during cold or windy weather and feel a draft, you have infiltration problems. In extreme cases the window frames rattle, and often the glass within the frames rattles, too. A typical 36-inch by 52-inch double hung window which, due to wear and tear, has a slight $1/16$-inch space around the sashes (the part that holds the panes) can create a huge dollar leak. Adding up that $1/16$ of an inch gap all the way around the perimeter of the window, you come out with a hole that measures $13\frac{1}{2}$ square inches. And anyone with a hole in the wall of $13\frac{1}{2}$ square inches can tell you it gets pretty cold during the winter. But that's only one window with normal wear and tear. The rest of your windows could very well be in the same condition and you could be throwing away money on heating or cooling the great outdoors. You can probably equate it to leaving one or more windows open all winter long and then trying to heat your home.

Installing windows and storms that fit tightly is imperative—especially the storm windows. To ensure this, weather stripping and caulking are used. For windows which are permanently sealed with thermopane, caulking is used both inside and out. But on double-hung windows with storms, weather stripping is used for movable sections and caulking is used for permanent areas.

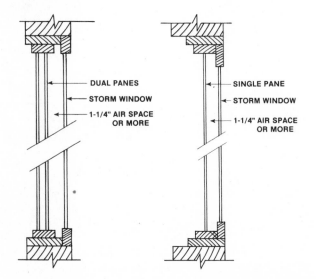

The diagrams show that storm windows must fit snugly, whether used with single or double-glazed windows, in order to be effective (Owens-Corning Fiberglas).

How to Buy Storm Windows

If your windows are in fairly good condition but are single-glazed, the easiest solution to the conduction problem is to add storm windows. The air between the storm window and the inside window may not be hermetically sealed as in double-glazed thermopane, but air is trapped between them and cuts heat loss in the same manner. Metal rather than wood frames are easier to handle and require less maintenance, but are less energy-efficient because they are conductors. If you feel that your windows are in such disrepair that they warrant replacement, look at double-glazed window replacements and follow directions given later in this chapter on how to install them.

Shown here are various types of windows and what to look for when purchasing storms for them.

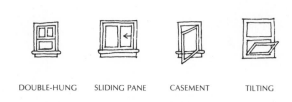

DOUBLE-HUNG   SLIDING PANE   CASEMENT   TILTING

Double-hung Window. By buying a storm and screen sash, you can simply slide the screen or storm window into place depending on the outside temperature. You can buy either two- or three-track units that are attached to the outside of your present window. Low cost units come with a single track, with a storm and screen in the same channel. The screen in this case has to be removed before the storm is inserted. With two-track units, one storm window and the screen are in the outer track while the other storm window is in the inner track. The storm slides up and down as the need dictates; the screen can be removed for storage or left in place. To allow more light to enter the room, it's best to remove and store screen. In a three-track unit, two storm windows and the screen all occupy different tracks so that moving one into place is simply a matter of sliding it in its track.

Sliding Window. A storm window or panel can be clipped to these units either on the inside or outside of the window. If attached to the outside window, weather stripping is usually required because there is no secondary seal. This system does not operate on tracks. The storm covers the entire window area and ventilation is achieved only when storm is removed.

Casement Window. Storm windows for this type of unit must be placed on the inside and attached to the sash. Obviously, once the storm window is in place you cannot get any ventilation until it is removed.

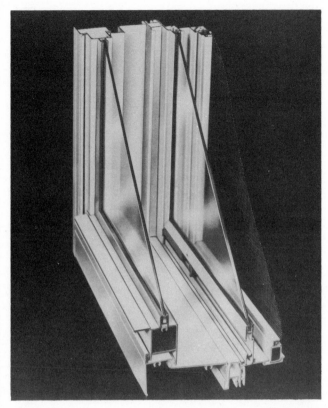

The three-track unit shown above is the easiest to use. Two storms (for upper and lower window) and a screen (for either upper or lower window) all occupy different tracks (Season-all Industries, Inc.).

Tilt Window. The storm window or panel is attached either to the outside or inside sash depending which way the window swings to open. If it opens out, storms are attached in a way similar to casement windows. If it opens inward, storms are attached like those on sliding windows. Ventilation is not possible in either case unless storms are completely removed.

No matter what type of window you have, when purchasing storm windows to fit them, you should beware of paying any money before you inspect the product. If you do decide to purchase storm windows the most expensive route is to have a contractor install them. A less expensive way is to buy the units and install them yourself. The least expensive solution is to make your own storm windows. All of these options will be fully described.

Purchasing Tips

Inspect the various types of storm windows carefully and look at the following points.

- Know the gauge of the metal frame. The heavier the gauge, the more substantial the quality for long-lasting units. This will mean a higher price, but it may be worth it. Make sure that the unit isn't overly light or bends with a slight touch. It won't last long and you'll probably be in the market for new units within two to four years.
- Note the finish of the metal frame. If it is plain aluminum, the finish will oxidize and cut down on ease of operation as well as appearance. An anodized or baked enamel finish is more suitable.
- Look at the corner joints. The corner should be overlapping and not mitered. This point of construction quality affects performance, strength and longevity of the unit. If you can see through the corners (on many cheaper units this is possible), you will have air infiltration problems.
- Inspect the depth of the metal grooves at the sides of the window; this and the weather stripping quality make a big difference in how well the storm window can stop air infiltration.
- Compare the quality of several different brands before selecting the one you want to install.
- Look closely at the locks and catches as a good indication of how well the unit is constructed.
- Watch out for poorly sealed joints where the two glass inserts (or insert) and screen meet. There should be a soft, tight seal.
- Test the inserts to see how they operate. They should slide in and out easily. If they are difficult to manipulate in the store, be extremely wary of buying them.

How To Install Storm Windows

For most homes the best add-on storm windows to buy and install are aluminum storm and screen units. Although the price varies considerably depending on quality and where you purchase the units, you can usually save about 10 percent to 15 percent by installing them yourself rather than hiring a contractor.

If you plan to do it yourself, set aside at least two weekends for the job. You won't need many tools, only a caulking gun, drill, and screw driver.

Before you purchase the windows, measure and then double check your outside dimensions to ensure that the windows will fit correctly. If your house is old, measure to see that the window frames are square. If they are not, you will have to buy a slightly smaller unit and then shim it with several wedges of wood.

Typical combination storm-and-screen windows are usually set in place in the window. Holes are drilled through the metal and into the window frame. Screws are then tightened down to hold the unit in place. Most combination units will come with two or three ¼-inch diameter holes (or other types of vents) drilled through the frame where it meets the window sill. This is to keep winter condensation from collecting on the sill and causing rot. Keep these holes clear, and drill them yourself if your units do not come predrilled.

Once the unit is installed, make sure that both the storm window and screen slide smoothly. If not, measure the unit for square. You can usually get the window working by loosening up on one or more of the screws holding the frame in place and shimming the unit. Finally caulk and weather strip the unit according to the directions at the end of this chapter.

Homemade Storm Windows

Obviously not everybody wants to make storm windows. If you plan a long-time stay and have the money, by all means purchase a good set of storm windows for your home. It is the least troublesome way and offers the best protection against heat loss and high bills. But if your budget doesn't permit the purchase of storm windows or you have a moving date set in your mind, neither your timetable nor your budget should override the obvious fact: YOU CAN NOT AFFORD TO BE WITHOUT STORM WINDOWS.

One way to resolve this problem is perhaps to buy one or two storm windows per year and seal up the rest of the windows for the winter with the homemade version. A big cash outlay is avoided and eventually you will have storms on all your windows.

In the meantime…you can make your own storm windows because the principle of using air as an insulator works as long as it is sealed between two layers of a material. As a matter of fact, making your own storms actually takes just a few minutes and costs under $1 per window.

The least expensive way to tackle this project is to first measure around the frame of the window. Once the dimensions are obtained, purchase the proper length of ½-inch quarter-round molding and a sheet of plastic. Cut the molding to the proper length and width and then place the plastic against the window frame. Tack the molding over it. Once this fast storm window is in place, caulk around the edges of the molding to prevent air infiltration. Care must be taken when installing this type of unit not to puncture the plastic. If the plastic is punctured, tape it to prevent air leaks. The molding and plastic can be purchased in any hardware and home center outlet. The tools you'll need include a hammer, saw, miter box and scissors. These "windows" last approximately one year.

Making your own storm windows with clear plastic takes a few minutes and costs under $1 per window. These will last one season (Dept. of Housing and Urban Development).

Although some homeowners make a more permanent type of storm window which is a bit more expensive, the end result doesn't usually justify the time or the money. In this type of make-it-yourself storm window, the wooden frame covered with the plastic is removable. It fits into the window unit and is taken down and stored during the warm months. But the quality of the wood that is purchased often results in extensive warpage the first year, which means that it is almost impossible to reinstall the following year. And most vinyl plastics degenerate in the sunlight, so that the material usually doesn't last well more than one year anyway.

Keeping Glass in Good Repair

It almost goes without saying that a key to keeping low heating bills starts with checking "loose" windows and those with cracked glass. Glass should be maintained in top condition all year. When you find a window with cracked glass, masking tape should be placed firmly over the crack until it can be repaired. It should then be repaired as soon as weather conditions permit.

How To Replace a Faulty Window

More than likely even if your home is considered old and you've repaired and repainted and refinished many parts of it, you haven't replaced the windows. If your windows are in poor condition, they can be weather stripped and you can add storms, but you'd probably be better off replacing the units altogether.

How can you tell when it's time to replace windows? Be on the lookout if your windows just don't seem to be doing what they're supposed to. Does the outside view seem blurry? Do you always have to prop your window open because it won't stay that way by itself? Do you constantly have to caulk and weather strip your windows because of the drafts? With enough "yes" answers to those questions, you might want to start thinking about installing new windows in place of the old ones. You may have reached the point of no return where your time and money on repairs simply aren't worth the investment.

Until a few years ago this was a very costly undertaking, but many window manufacturers today are offering custom-fit windows which require no structural alteration. Many of these companies can be found in the directory at the back of the book. By following the illustrations here, you should be able to do the job efficiently.

Then remove sash.

Remove window trim to free sash.

Using screwdriver for leverage, remove wooden channels and all other obstructions.

Assemble new unit according to manufacturers instructions. The next three photos show how one unit goes together.

When unit is assembled, make sure that it fits squarely into the space. If space is not square use wooden shims to make window fit. Do not bend frame to make it fit space!

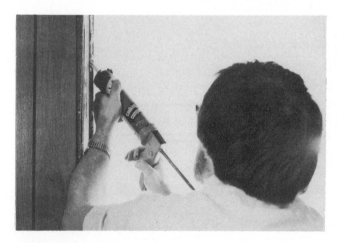

Remove window and apply generous amount of caulking before installation.

Set window into opening and tighten down screw at one corner. Then square and plumb unit for final adjustment.

Fasten remaining sections of window in place as shown in next two photos. As you tighten down the screws, make sure you do not bend the unit to meet the wall. If wall is warped, use a shim behind window to maintain square.

Caulk between new window and inside wall.

Install sashes according to manufacturer's instructions.

Put up new molding unit around window. (Photos courtesy of Season-all Industries, Inc.).

DOORS

Doors are usually more energy-efficient than windows but they still can cost you money. Similar to windows, doors suffer from problems such as air infiltration and conduction. Air infiltration is the major problem. Doors open. And small children often leave them that way, so that your heating bill soars along with your temper. You can figure spending 5 percent to 10 percent more on heating or cooling bills than necessary. Of course if you have more than four children plus a cat and a dog, you could be spending 15 percent of your energy dollars on them. Obviously, descriptions of saving money on your energy bills in this chapter must include training everyone in your home to keep the door shut while the heating or cooling system is running.

Air Infiltration

Doors on the typical single-family home are usually solid-core wood (doors mentioned in this chapter are all doors which lead outside). The average door which is about 1¾ inches thick has an R-value of about 2 (your well-insulated wall has an R-value of 15). If you happen to have a hollow core door to the exterior, it should be replaced immediately! Not many homes have exterior hollow core doors but it will pay to check anyway.

Like windows, the only way to increase your R-value is to add another layer with air in between. The typical solution is a storm door. A substantial wooden storm door will increase the R-value about 3.5 to 4, depending on the amount of glass in the storm door. (Most have about 50 percent glass, possibly to show the features of the primary door). Aluminum storm doors will increase the R-value to about 3.

Some doors which are made of several pieces of wood often have air leaks within the unit. Others leak around the door frame. But besides adding a storm door, the units must also be "tight." Weather stripping must be added around the door for best results. As in windows, the air infiltration problem may also require caulking (unlike the movable sections which take weather stripping around the door frame). Weather stripping and caulking instructions are at the end of this chapter. To buy and install a storm door, follow the same instructions as for windows.

Doors As Windows

Should doors be used as windows? This question is being asked more frequently, since builders and architects have increased the use of sliding glass doors. In terms of saving dollars on your energy bill, the answer (based on our information) is "no."

In areas specifically designed for windows, a window should be used. And if ventilation isn't required, a fixed glass window may be the best solution for getting natural light and/or a good view in the room. You may then place a door in the room if it is required.

There are times, however, when sliding glass doors can be beneficial. That is when space is at a premium and both light and the view are also overriding factors. But in all cases when contemplating sliding glass doors you should only consider thermopane ones. This may increase the original purchase price, but in the long run—not too long at that—your heating or cooling bills will more than make up for the difference.

HOW TO WEATHER STRIP WINDOWS AND DOORS

To weather strip your windows and doors you'll need a hammer, nails, screwdriver, tin snips and tape measure. It usually takes less than one-half hour per window. You have a choice of installing at least three different types of weather stripping.

Metal strip

This strip is installed into the channel of the window or door so that it is virtually invisible. Because this weather stripping is metal, it is very durable. It doesn't need much maintenance but is somewhat difficult to install. Costs about $2 per window.

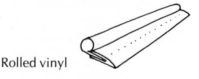

Rolled vinyl

It is available with or without metal backing; is durable, easy to install, but visible. Costs under $2 per window.

Foam rubber with adhesive backing

The least expensive, it is extremely easy to install but is also the least durable. It breaks down quickly, particularly where friction occurs, so you may be back weather stripping next autumn. Cost is pennies per foot.

Thin spring metal

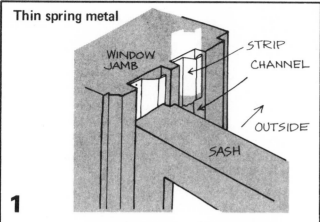

1

Install by moving sash to the open position and sliding strip in between the sash and the channel. Tack in place into the casing. Do not cover the pulleys in the upper channels.

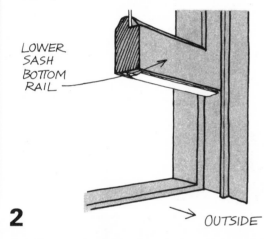

2

Install strips the full width of the sash on the bottom of the lower sash bottom rail and the top of the upper sash top rail.

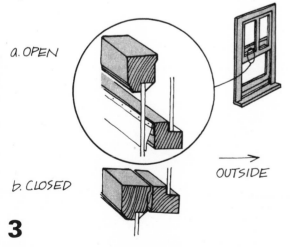

3

Then attach a strip the full width of the window to the upper sash bottom rail. Countersink the nails slightly so they won't catch on the lower sash top rail.

Source: Dept. of Housing and Urban Development.

Rolled vinyl

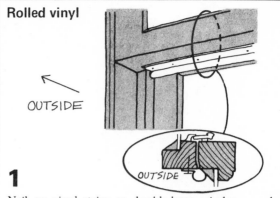

1

Nail on vinyl strips on double-hung windows as shown. A sliding window is much the same and can be treated as a double-hung window turned on its side. Casement and

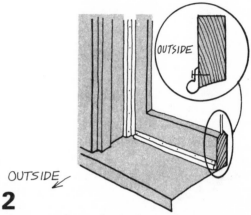

2

tilting windows should be weatherstripped with the vinyl nailed to the window casing so that, as the window shuts, it compresses the roll.

Adhesive-backed foam strip

Install adhesive backed foam, on all types of windows, only where there is no friction. On double-hung windows, this is only on the bottom (as shown) and top rails. Other types of windows can use foam strips in many more places.

WEATHERSTRIP YOUR DOORS

AN EASY DO-IT-YOURSELF PROJECT

You can weatherstrip your doors even if you're not an experienced handyman. There are several types of weatherstripping for doors, each with its own level of effectiveness, durability and degree of installation difficulty. Select among the options given the one you feel is best for you. The installations are the same for the two sides and top of a door, with a different, more durable one for the threshold.

The Alternative Methods and Materials

1. Adhesive backed foam:

Tools

Knife or shears,
Tape measure

Evaluation — extremely easy to install, invisible when installed, not very durable, more effective on doors than windows.

Installation — stick foam to inside face of jamb.

2. Rolled vinyl with aluminum channel backing:

Tools

Hammer, nails,
Tin snips
Tape measure

Evaluation — easy to install, visible when installed, durable.

Installation — nail strip snugly against door on the casing

3. Foam rubber with wood backing:

Tools

Hammer, nails,
Hand saw,
Tape measure

Evaluation — easy to install, visible when installed, not very durable.

Installation — nail strip snugly against the closed door. Space nails 8 to 12 inches apart.

4. Spring metal:

Tools

Tin snips
Hammer, nails,
Tape measure

Evaluation — easy to install, invisible when installed, extremely durable.

Installation — cut to length and tack in place. Lift outer edge of strip with screwdriver after tacking, for better seal.

Note: These methods are harder than 1 through 4.

5. Interlocking metal channels:

Tools

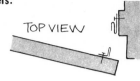

TOP VIEW

Hack saw,
Hammer, nails,
Tape measure

Evaluation — difficult to install (alignment is critical), visible when installed, durable but subject to damage, because they're exposed, excellent seal.

Installation — cut and fit strips to head of door first: male strip on door, female on head; then hinge side of door: male strip on jamb, female on door; finally lock side on door, female on jamb.

6. Fitted interlocking metal channels: (J-Strips)

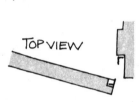

TOP VIEW

Evaluation — very difficult to install, exceptionally good weather seal, invisible when installed, not exposed to possible damage.

Installation — should be installed by a carpenter. Not appropriate for do-it-yourself installation unless done by an accomplished handyman.

7. Sweeps:

INSIDE

Tools

Screwdriver,
Hack saw,
Tape measure

Evaluation — useful for flat threshholds, may drag on carpet or rug.

Installation — cut sweep to fit 1/16 inch in from the edges of the door. Some sweeps are installed on the inside and some outside. Check instructions for your particular type.

8. Door Shoes:

Tools

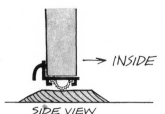

INSIDE

SIDE VIEW

Screwdriver,
Hack saw,
Plane,
Tape measure

Evaluation — useful with wooden threshhold that is not worn, very durable, difficult to install (must remove door).

Installation — remove door and trim required amount off bottom. Cut to door width. Install by sliding vinyl out and fasten with screws.

9. Vinyl bulb threshold:

Tools

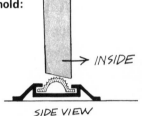

INSIDE

SIDE VIEW

Screwdriver,
Hack saw,
Plane,
Tape measure

Evaluation — useful where there is no threshhold or wooden one is worn out, difficult to install, vinyl will wear but replacements are available.

Installation — remove door and trim required amount off bottom. Bottom should have about 1/8" bevel to seal against vinyl. Be sure bevel is cut in right direction for opening.

10. Interlocking threshold:

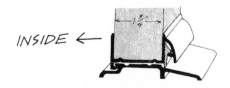

INSIDE ←

Evaluation — very difficult to install, exceptionally good weather seal.

Installation — should be installed by a skilled carpenter.

Source: Dept. of Housing and Urban Development.

CAULKING

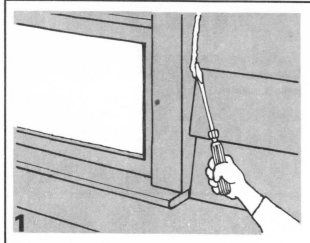

1 Before applying caulking compound, clean area of paint build-up, dirt, or deteriorated caulk with solvent and putty knife or large screwdriver.

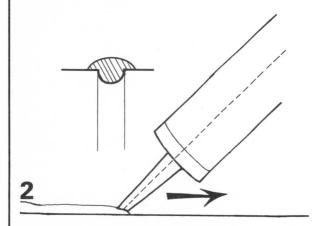

2 Drawing a good bead of caulk will take a little practice. First attempts may be a bit messy. Make sure the bead overlaps both sides for a tight seal.

3 A wide bead may be necessary to make sure caulk adheres to both sides.

4 Fill extra wide cracks like those at the sills (where the house meets the foundation) with oakum, glass fiber insulation strips, etc.)

FOUNDATION SILL

5 In places where you can't quite fill the gaps, finish the job with caulk.

6 Caulking compound also comes in rope form. Unwind it and force it into cracks with your fingers. You can fill extra long cracks easily this way.

Source: Dept. of Housing and Urban Development.

Weather stripping is purchased by the running foot. You can estimate your weather stripping simply by measuring the perimeter around one window. If all your windows are the same size, multiply the perimeter number by the amount of windows you have to weather strip. The same procedure is followed for doors. If necessary you may have to measure each window and/or door and come up with the total footage. Then add anywhere from 5 percent to 10 percent for waste and you will know how many feet of weather stripping you should purchase.

CAULKING WINDOWS AND DOORS

Caulking materials are available in most hardware and home center stores in three types: oil or resin base caulk; latex, butyl or polyvinyl based caulk; and elastomeric caulks. Don't pinch pennies when buying caulk, and spread it around generously over surfaces that need it.

An oil or resin base caulk will bond to any surface; it is not very durable but it is the cheapest. The latex, butyl or polyvinyl caulk will bond to most surfaces. It will last longer but it is more expensive. The elastomeric caulks are the most durable and the most expensive.

So that a massive amount of caulk is not wasted for large cracks, secure the oakum, caulking cotton, and sponge rubber to fill in cracks before caulking. When estimating how much caulk to purchase, figure about ½ cartridge per window.

Follow the illustrations and instructions given here for caulking.

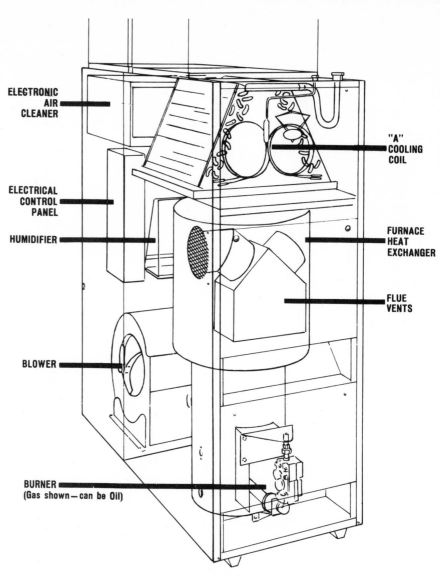

ELECTRONIC
AIR
CLEANER

"A"
COOLING
COIL

ELECTRICAL
CONTROL
PANEL

HUMIDIFIER

FURNACE
HEAT
EXCHANGER

FLUE
VENTS

BLOWER

BURNER
(Gas shown — can be Oil)

Modern forced warm-air furnaces are very popular; this one heats with gas (Dept. of Agriculture).

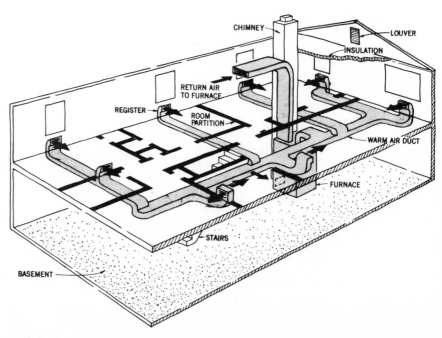

CHIMNEY

LOUVER

INSULATION

RETURN AIR
TO FURNACE

REGISTER

ROOM
PARTITION

WARM AIR DUCT

FURNACE

STAIRS

BASEMENT

With this forced warm-air system, you are able to combine a cooling system with the same unit (Dept. of Agriculture).

3. Heating and Cooling

Heating and cooling bills are high now and can account for 60 percent of your energy costs. They will go higher. You can save money by buying an efficient heating and/or cooling system to serve your needs, or fix your system to get the most out of it.

FUELS

The major problem with selecting a new heating system and the main impetus for energy conservation today, are the price and availability of fuels for home heating. All fuels are expensive, but *natural gas* (supplied by pipe lines to the burner under low pressure) which is price-controlled by the Federal Government, is the only "bargain" around. Unfortunately in many localities east of the Mississippi, gas is not available for new hookups and areas west of the River where gas is available are diminishing daily. Natural gas is extremely convenient to use; it takes up no storage space, and requires no handling.

Oil

This popular form of home-heating fuel is available but is subject to the whims of international oil interests, which could make the fuel either hard to obtain or a great deal more expensive on short notice. The advantages are: it requires little space for storage and no handling.

Wood and Coal

These are readily available but the handling and storing difficulties involved make them undesirable for the typical American family.

Electricity

Although expensive and getting more expensive, electricity is readily available. In fact, energy experts in and out of government "conservatively" predict that the prices of all fuels will rise between 10 percent and 12 percent well into the future. And with fossil fuels becoming scarcer as the years go on, this does not bode well for anyone. Users of electricity for heating, especially in areas of the East where the price of a kilowatt hour is 8¢ or more, are ex-periencing heating bills in excess of $1,000 per year. These unfortunate homeowners have one of several forms of electric-resistance heating. It is strongly suggested that almost any other fuel be used over this form of electric heating.

CHOOSING A NEW HEATING SYSTEM

If you need a new heating system for your present home or are investigating possibilities for a new home, there are a number of standard systems to choose from. You should of course be influenced by the energy costs in your area.

Forced Warm Air

This system consists of a furnace, ducts, and registers. A blower in the furnace circulates the warm air to the various rooms through supply ducts and registers. Return grilles and ducts carry the cooled room air back to the furnace where it is reheated and recirculated.

This system heats uniformly and responds rapidly to changes in outdoor temperatures. It can be used in houses with or without basements—the furnace need not be below the rooms to be heated, nor centrally located. Some can be adapted for summer cooling by the addition of cooling coils. Combination heating-and-cooling systems may be installed. The same ducts can be used for both heating and cooling.

The warm air is usually filtered through inexpensive replaceable or washable filters. Electronic air cleaners can sometimes be installed in existing systems and are available on specially designed furnaces for new installations. These remove pollen, fine dust, and other irritants that get through ordinary filters.

A humidifier may be added to the system to add moisture to the house air and avoid the discomfort and other disadvantages of too-dry air (See Chapter 4 on ventilation).

Warm air supply outlets are preferably located along outside walls. They should be low in the wall, in the baseboard, or in the floor where air cannot blow directly on the room occupants. Floor registers tend to collect dust and trash, but may have to be used when installing a new system in an old house.

Hot-water and Steam Heat

Hot-water and steam heating systems consist of a boiler, pipes, and room heating units (radiators or convectors). Hot water or steam is generated in the boiler, and circulates through the pipes to the radiators or convectors where the heat is transferred to the room air.

Boilers are made of cast iron or steel and are designed for burning coal, gas, or oil. Cast-iron boilers are more resistant to corrosion than steel ones. Corrosive water can be improved with chemicals. Proper water treatment can greatly prolong the life of steel boiler tubes.

If you are interested in such a system, only certified boilers should be purchased. Certified cast-iron are stamped "I-B-R" (Institute of Boiler Radiator Manufacturers); steel boilers are stamped "SBI" (Steel Boiler Institute). Most boilers are rated—on the nameplate—for both hot water and steam. Contractors should be contacted when selecting a new boiler.

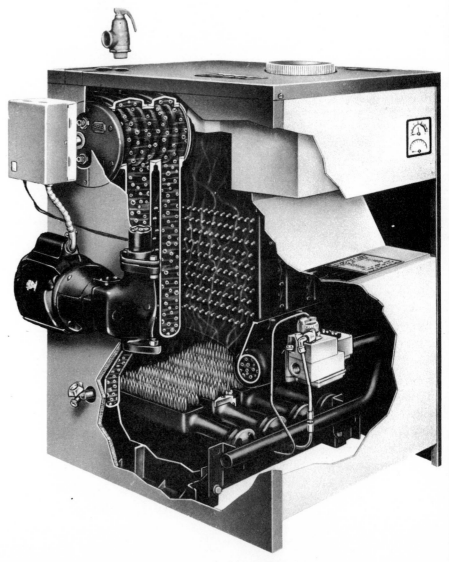

Gas boiler is a compact self-contained unit (Dept. of Agriculture).

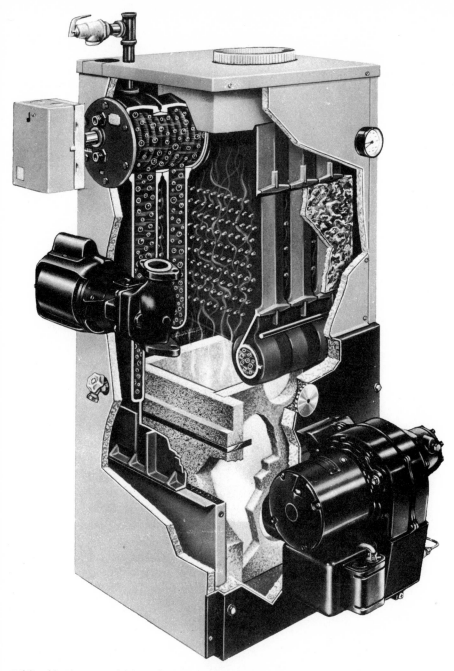

Oil fired boiler is available with completely enclosed jacket (Dept. of Agriculture).

Radiators. Conventional radiators are set on the floor or mounted on the wall. The newer types may be recessed in the wall. (Insulate behind recessed units with one inch of insulation board, a sheet of reflective insulation or, better yet, both.) Radiators may be partially or fully enclosed in a cabinet. A full cabinet must have openings at top and bottom for air circulation. Preferred locations for radiators are under windows. Baseboard radiators are hollow or finned units that resemble and are placed near conventional wood baseboard along outside walls. They will heat a well-insulated room uniformly with little temperature variation between floor and ceiling.

Convectors. These usually consist of finned tubes enclosed in a cabinet with openings at the top and bottom. They are installed against an outside wall or recessed into the wall. Hot water or steam circulates through the tubes, and goes out the top. Some units have fans for forced air circulation. With this type of convector, summer cooling may be provided by adding a chiller and the necessary controls to the system.

Radiant-panel Heat. This is another method of heating with forced hot water, steam or electricity. Hot water or steam circulates through pipes concealed in the floor, wall or ceiling. Heat is transmitted through pipes to the surface of the floor, wall or ceiling and then to the room

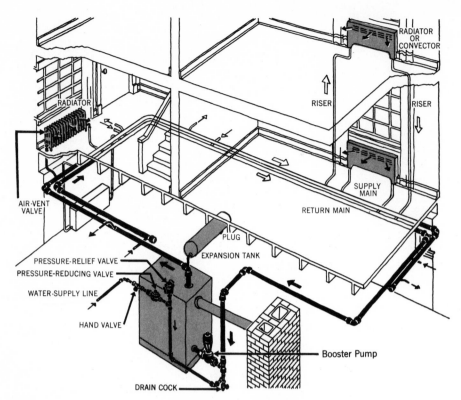

Two-pipe forced hot-water system has one pipe supplying hot water to the room-heating units while the other pipe returns cooled water to the boiler (Dept. of Agriculture).

by radiation and convection. No radiators are required—the floor, wall or ceiling, in effect, acts as a radiator. With radiant-panel heating, rooms can be more comfortable at lower temperatures than with other heating systems at higher air temperatures. The reason is that the radiated heat striking the room occupant reduces body heat loss and increases body comfort. Temperatures are generally uniform throughout the house.

Forced Warm-water Heat.

This system is recommended over the less-efficient gravity hot-water heating systems just described. In a forced warm-water system, a small booster or circulating pump forces or circulates the hot water through the pipes to the room radiators or convectors.

In a one-pipe system, one pipe (or main) serves for both supply and return. It makes a complete circuit from the boiler and back again. Two risers extend from the main to each room-heating unit. In a two-pipe system, one pipe carries the heated water to the room heating units, the other pipe returns the cooled water to the boiler.

A one-pipe system, as the name implies, takes less pipe than a two-pipe system, but you should be aware of the following. In the one-pipe system, cooled water from each radiator mixes with the hot water flowing through the main and each succeeding radiator receives cooler water. Allowance must be made for this in sizing the radiators—larger ones may be required further along the system.

Electric Heating

Many types and designs of electric house heating equipment are available. Some are: (1) ceiling units (2) baseboard heaters (3) heat pumps (4) central furnace (5) wall units. Resistance heaters (space heaters) produce heat the same way as the familiar portable electric heater.

Ceiling heat is created with an electric heating cable laid back and forth on the ceiling surface. It is covered with plaster or a second layer of gypsum board. Other types of ceiling heaters include infrared lamps and resistance heaters with reflectors or fans.

Electric heating cable usually located in the ceiling is one of several different types of electric heat (Dept. of Agriculture).

Baseboard heaters resemble ordinary baseboards and are often used under a large picture window in conjunction with ceiling heat.

The heat pump is a single unit that both heats and cools. In winter it takes heat from the outdoor air to warm the house or room. Sometimes heat pumps use water in the ground to exchange heat rather than using the outside air. In summer it removes heat from the house or room and discharges it to the outside air. It uses less electricity to furnish the same amount of heat than does the resistance-type heater. Room air conditioners of the heat-pump type are convenient in warm climates.

Resistance heaters are used in forced air central furnace heating systems. This system requires ducts similar to those mentioned in forced warm air heating. An electric hot-water heating system with resistance heaters is also available but it is extremely expensive to operate.

Wall units, either radiant or convection, or both, are designed for recessed or surface wall mounting. They come equipped with various types of resistance heating elements. The warm air may be circulated either by gravity or by an electric fan.

Heat pump can absorb heat even during cold weather. At temperatures of 15 degrees, the heat pump switches off and resistance electric heat takes over (General Electric Co.).

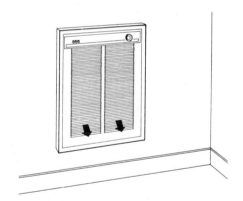

Popular types of electric wall heaters are located near the floor and discharge warm air into room by means of fans, an example of convection (Dept. of Agriculture).

The Heat Pump

One form of electric heating that is rapidly gaining in popularity is the heat pump, which can cut electric heat bills by 40 percent! Until very recently the heat pump had a dubious reputation. Its ability to save on electricity was recognized but many of the heat pump units on sale were unreliable. Today, that has all changed, and units produced by the top manufacturers are as reliable as other heating systems.

The heat pump works on the same principle as the common household variety refrigerator or air conditioner. Heat is transferred from one place or source at a relatively low temperature to another at a higher temperature. The most widely used heat pump is the so-called air-to-air unit. It absorbs heat from one source of air and discharges it into another.

The two basic types of air-to-air units which can be purchased are: a single package unit, and a split system. The single package unit comes with compressor, two heat exchanger coils (evaporator and condenser), two fans or blowers, and electrical controls in one unit. The split system has one part on the outside of the house and the other on the inside. On the inside is one heat exchanger coil, fan and controls; on the outside, a heat exchanger coil, fan and compressor. These two parts connect by means of a pipe which carries a refrigerant such as Freon from outside to inside to outside.

The heat pump is both a heating and cooling machine and would replace both the furnace and a central air conditioner in a typical home. During the cooling cycle, when the house must be air conditioned, cold refrigerant is pumped into the inside heat exchanger coil. A fan blows air from the house across this coil and heats up the refrigerant. Because the refrigerant absorbs heat, it cools off the air.

This refrigerant is a very volatile fluid and as it absorbs heat it evaporates into a gas inside the coil. This hot gas flows out of the house then and into a compressor. The compressor, as its name implies, compresses this hot gas into a super-heated liquid. The hot liquid then flows to the outside heat exchanger coil where another fan blows air across it to remove the heat from the liquid and cool it off.

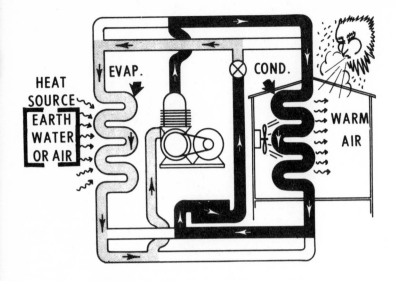

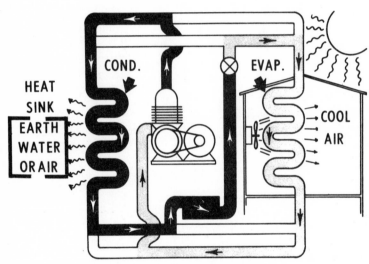

The two cycles of the heat pump as shown above. Top shows heating cycle while bottom illustrates cooling cycle (Dept. of Agriculture).

During the heating cycle just the opposite occurs. Heat is absorbed from the outside air even at temperatures as low as 15 degrees. This heat is pumped into the house, the inside blower pushes air across it, removing heat from the coil and heating the inside space.

The big interest during these times of high fuel prices is that a heat pump system works at great efficiency. When you pay your electric bill you are actually paying for kilowatt hours of electricity which you used. Prices range from as little as 3¢ to 8¢ or more per kwh. The heat pump runs on electricity. But for every BTU unit you purchase while running the heat pump you are gaining between 2 and 3 BTU units from the outside air for nothing. The heat pump during the heating cycle is most efficient at 45 or 50 degrees and its efficiency diminishes as the

temperature drops. At 50 degrees you might have an efficiency of 3 while at 20 degrees you might have an efficiency of 2. Even at this efficiency however, the heat pump is cheaper to operate than typical resistance heating.

On days when the temperature drops below 15 degrees, the heat pump switches off and resistance heat comes on. Resistance heat is not as efficient but the cost differential in the energy you use with heat pumps at very low temperatures is not worth the wear and tear on the heat pump parts.

Climate zones. Heat pumps have been used quite successfully in the south for the last decade or so. For this reason, it has gained a reputation for being a "southern" heating and cooling system. This is not so. The heat pump can be used in very cold climates. Obviously, if in the winter the temperatures stay below 15 degrees in your area, the heat pump will be of little use. In most parts of the U.S. however, the average temperature is usually in the 30 degree range or higher. In these climates, the heat pump is very effective.

Cost. There are several things that must be taken into account when considering a heat pump. If only heating is desired, the heat pump will not be economical from a first-cost standpoint. It would be like paying for the installation of a heating and central air conditioning system and then just using the heating part.

The second consideration is that if natural gas is available, use it. It is still cheaper to heat with gas than a heat pump. With other types of fuel, however, the heat pump is competitive. Studies show that the heat pump uses less fuel than other heating and cooling systems. If you can handle the first cost of a heat pump, you can expect considerable fuel savings over the years which will help pay for the unit. A heat pump for a new home will probably run between 20 and 25 percent more than other heating and cooling units. That is, if another heating and cooling unit cost $2,000 installed, the heat pump will run between $2,400 to $2,500.

As an example of possible savings: a major builder in the Washington, D.C. area until two years ago had used electrical-resistance heat in his homes. His customers started to complain that heating bills were topping $200 a month during the heating season, so he shifted to heat pumps. The results of the first few winters revealed that the heat pump cut this monthly cost between 40 and 45 percent. In this case, the heat pump cost more originally but it paid for itself in about three years.

Another reason to look into a heat pump is that as the years go on, the natural efficiency of the heat pump will help hold down increasingly higher energy bills. If it costs you $200 for monthly heating, the heat pump could save you about $80. If the fuel price increases 50 percent in another five years, the heat pump would be saving $120.

If you are stuck with resistance heat and high energy bills right now and cannot move, a heat pump might still be worth investigating. It would cost substantially more to have one installed in an existing home, particularly if ductwork had to be installed, but it still might be worth it.

Because heat pumps are relatively new as far as the public is concerned, try to find a competent contractor in the area who has had experience installing the units. Go one step further and get the names of some of his customers to determine whether or not a good dollar savings is possible in your climate.

A good source of heat pump manufacturers is located at the end of this book. You can also write to the Air Conditioning and Refrigeration Institute (1815 Fort Myer Dr., Arlington, Virginia 22209) for a directory of certified heat pump manufacturers.

Maintenance on heat pumps is very different from other heating systems. This machine is a highly tuned piece of equipment which needs an expert. *Do not try to maintain it yourself.* If the system gets out of whack, compressor failure could result and this could cost hundreds of dollars to replace. Either through the manufacturer or a competent contractor, you can buy a service contract for around $80 to keep the system in top order.

HEATING SYSTEMS IN EXISTING HOMES

Production of heated or cooled air for your home accounts for the bulk of energy consumed each year. If you don't plan to move or to purchase new equipment, any increase in efficiency in your old heating system will be reflected in the family budget the first year. Although use of heating and air conditioning varies from section to section in the U.S., on a national basis we use about eleven times more energy for heating than for air conditioning. Even with older heating equipment you can cut costs by (1) checking your thermostat, (2) balancing your heating system, (3) tuning up and servicing your equipment, and (4) managing your system efficiently.

Thermostat

Some families keep their homes too warm in the winter and too cool in the summer. The same family member who does not feel snug and warm in the winter unless the thermostat is set at 75 degrees is likely to feel "too hot" in the summer unless the air conditioner is maintained at 68 degrees. You should try for just the opposite for lower energy bills. Big dollars can be saved by maintaining a 68 degree temperature in the winter and a 75 degree temperature in the summer. How much? Recent estimates put the amount of heating energy waste at between 3 and 5 percent of the annual energy bill for every degree that the temperature is maintained over 68 degrees.

If you maintain a 75 degree temperature in your home in the winter and your heating bill is $400 for the season, those extra degrees are costing you around 25 percent or $100 of the bill. If your annual heating bill is $600 or $800 you are paying a lot more for those extra few degrees. Similar dollars are wasted with an air conditioner kept too low. The thermostat, therefore, becomes your first line of defense against high energy bills.

Besides keeping the thermostat too high, another problem which can add a great deal to the energy bill is the household "juggler." This is the person who turns the thermostat up or down depending on how he or she feels for the moment. If the juggler is a little chilly, up goes the thermostat. If the juggler is too warm, either the thermostat is turned back down, or worse yet, the window is opened! Every time the heating system comes on and the room becomes warm, the juggler becomes "hot" and decides to lower the temperature. Then the heating system shuts off and the ducts, the furnace, and the flue which are hot, rapidly cool off and waste their heat. Now the juggler feels cold and turns up the thermostat. When the system comes on, all these same parts must heat up again before the room warms up. The constant juggling of the thermostat could add considerably to your annual heating bill.

There has been no device yet created to lock the thermostat at one temperature, but household members can be educated. If someone feels chilly, they should put on heavier clothing. Americans have gotten into the habit of wearing summer clothing inside the house no matter what the temperature is outside. In the summer, light clothing should be worn, and in the winter, heavier materials should be used.

Of course, if there are older people or babies living in the house, you would want to be less rigid with thermostat settings. Older people become chilled more quickly and special consideration must be made for them.

Balancing the Heating System

Most American homes have a central heating system usually located in basements or garages. There are several basic parts to every central heating system, as shown in the illustration at the opening of this chapter.

An unbalanced system can turn even the nicest household member into a thermostat juggler. A poorly adjusted heat distribution system creates uneven heat throughout the house. Typically, a student studying in one part of the house may be cold because it is only 65 degrees while his sister can feel uncomfortable in a 75 degree room in another area of the house. Even though you have educated everyone to leave the thermostat alone, one person might turn it up to gain heat while another tries to adjust it downward.

No matter what type of heating system you have, you can balance it. To balance the system you will need at least one room thermometer. On a cold day when the heating system is on, bring one thermometer into the room where the thermostat is located. See if you get the same reading on both. You can then be sure that comparing one part of the house to another will be done accurately. If the thermostat and thermometer vary, compensate on your thermometer readings in other parts of the house.

The way to balance these systems is to set the thermostat at a comfortable temperature (68 degrees), then take your thermometer readings in each room. You can adjust your system up or down until comparable temperatures are obtained in all areas of your home. Two different methods of balancing heating systems are used. One is used for steam and hot-water systems while another is required for hot air. (Electric space heating systems are not included in this section because usually each room or area has a separate thermostat which can easily be adjusted up or down according to thermometer readings.)

Steam and hot-water systems. These systems are adjustable by turning up the radiator valves, permitting more heat in the room, or turning them down for less heat. Some hot-water systems are zoned for certain areas of the house. The valve adjustments may be found in the basement near the furnace. But if your radiators do not have valves and you cannot find the valve system in the basement, you should install valves. Check with your plumbing supply house for properly sized valves and installation instructions. These valves can usually be purchased for a few dollars.

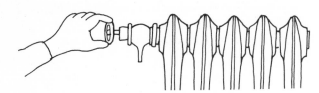

Adjust valves on hot water or steam system for heat control and balancing (Dept. of Housing and Urban Development).

Hot air system. There are five steps involved in balancing this type of system.

(1) On a cold day, turn the thermostat to the temperature desired. Then open all dampers in every room to the maximum. In rooms where the door is usually left open or closed, leave it that way. You want your system to be balanced to the normal functioning of your household.

(2) After 30 minutes to an hour, measure the temperature in each room with the thermometer. (If you use more than one thermometer, make sure they give similar readings.) Place it about two feet from the floor near the center of the room.

(3) Rooms which are too hot should have the damper closed somewhat. Reducing the heat flow in the overly hot rooms will increase it to the cooler ones.

(4) After cutting the heat to rooms which are hot, wait about an hour and measure the temperature again. When you cut a damper in one room, you must remeasure the temperature in each room to see how the heat is redistributed.

(5) Continue adjustments until you get a system which is balanced. Rooms which are unused should have the dampers closed all the way so heat gets to the places where it is needed more. *Do not close more than 20 percent of the dampers.* This could cause your heating system to fail, resulting in a high repair bill.

Tuning and Servicing

Just as your car needs to be tuned occasionally to keep it running efficiently, so must your heating system receive similar attention. Gas-fired units have few moving parts and need very little attention. Oil burners are very reliable but should be serviced at least once a year, preferably before the heating season. There is a good rule to follow on heating systems which is: If you don't know what you're doing, don't do it. There are, however, a number of things you can do. (If you prefer to have a serviceperson do them for around $30 or $40 a year, fine. Often service contracts are available for less.)

Filters. In forced hot-air systems dirty or clogged filters will cause your heating system to overwork and burn more fuel. Usually the filter is located in the front panel of the furnace. By removing this panel you can usually expose the filter and the other mechanisms of the unit. The filter can be changed quickly. If you are unsure how to do it, have a serviceperson come in the first time. Watch how it's done and then do it yourself in the future. Filters can be purchased for under a dollar and in packs of 10 or 12 for several dollars. They are available at any well stocked hardware store or home center.

Blowers. In forced hot-air systems the blower machinery needs lubrication. Some of the better units are permanently sealed and lubricated. You need to do nothing. Other units come with grease cups which must be resupplied with grease as needed. You should check your operating manual to determine exactly where it should be greased or oiled. If you are unsure, again bring in a serviceperson and watch what he does. There are belt-driven blowers which need the belts changed occasionally. Although they last for years, it is a good idea to check the belt and make sure it is tight. Also check the condition of the belt. If it is frayed or cracked, replace it.

Furnace motor. In a hot water system this unit needs lubricating oil, but not a lot. A few drops of oil two or three times a year is sufficient. It goes without saying that you should never get any oil on a fan belt. If you do, make sure you remove all the oil.

Duct system. In forced hot-air systems, if you have let your filters get dirty there could be a considerable buildup of dust in the grilles and duct work. They can be vacuumed out with your household vacuum cleaner. Every now and then you should have the entire duct system cleaned professionally. Service people have a special vacuum system for this job.

Your heating system should be checked by professionals. Unless you are a trained heating serviceperson, do not do it. A serviceperson will check the mixture of oil and air which is ignited by a powerful electrical current at electrodes. These electrodes must be perfectly adjusted for maximum efficiency. Only a qualified serviceperson can do this.

Managing Your Heating System Efficiently

As mentioned previously, your thermostat is your first line of defense against high energy bills. The thermostat is also the key in overall management of your heating system to reduce annual bills. Keep these tips in mind.

- Keep heat-producing items (lamps, TV, etc.) at least three feet from the thermostat. They may cause your thermostat to keep your home uncomfortably cool.
- Locate thermostat away from drafts so the furnace won't continue to run when the rest of the house is warm enough.
- Most new homes with fireplaces have dampers to close off the flue. Make sure the flue is always closed when heat is running. If you do not have a flue, invest in one—or fit it with something to prevent heat escaping up the cavity.
- Turn your thermostat down every opportunity you have. A five-degree set-back overnight (about 8 hours) will save 7 percent off your energy bill. A heating energy savings of approximately 11 percent can be attained by reducing thermostat setting 10 degrees from the normal night-time setting for a period of 8 hours. Of course if you will be gone for longer periods of time, turn your thermostat as low as possible as long as freezing is not possible inside.
- If you have an electric blanket, use it. These use much less energy than keeping your heating system running at daytime settings during the night.
- When you come into the house, do not turn the thermostat up to 85 degrees to heat the house "faster." The heating system works on a certain heat output. That is, it will put out 100,000 of BTU's per hour; turning up the thermostat won't change this output. You may, however, forget the thermostat was turned up and the house could heat up to 85 degrees before you notice your forgetfulness. That's a lot of money wasted.
- When entertaining a large group during the heating season, it is wise to lower the thermostat a degree or two before guests arrive. People generate heat and the room may become overheated, forcing you to open a window.
- Shut off unused rooms and close heating vents to these areas.
- If you have a fireplace, it may be causing your heating system to overwork. A good chimney can draw about 20 percent of the air out of the house per hour. During heating season keep damper closed unless fireplace is used! Most fireplaces are for your own personal enjoyment and most should not be used for supplemental heat (see Chapter 6) on severely cold days.
- Draw drapes over glass doors and windows to create a heat barrier (see Chapter 2) to reduce heat loss.
- Exhaust fans in the kitchen and bath which are ducted to the outside remove heated or cooled air. Use them with discretion.
- In arranging furniture, be careful not to block heating units. Drapes which cover heating registers or restrict air flow should be shortened. Baseboard heating units need air circulation in order to operate properly.
- Keep your heating system running at peak efficiency with checks and cleanings.
- If you have a gas or oil burner used to heat your house, between 25 and 50 percent of the fuel you purchase may be lost up the flue. On cold days if you look at the flue on your roof, you will see heat being lost into the air. There is a way to get this back before you heat the outdoors. A flue heat exchanger can be built into your furnace's flue which will pull the heat out of the pipe before it is lost outside. These units range in price between $100 and $150. In the typical unit you can recapture about 10 to 15 percent of your heat, which helps reduce the overall heating bill proportionately.

Many other tips to save on the use of your system are discussed in other sections of this book. Many are simply common sense. For instance, during sunny winter days, let the sun's light into your house to help ease the burden on the heating system. Or keep windows and doors closed as much as possible.

AIR CONDITIONING SYSTEMS

The very best way to save money on air conditioning is not to use it at all. But in some parts of the country and during some times of the year, air conditioning can be as vital as heating. In all cases, however, it should be used sparingly. When the day begins to cool off, the system should be shut off and the windows opened to take advantage of the cooler air.

The Attic Fan

One feasible alternative to air conditioning is the attic fan. An attic fan can draw radiant heat out before it filters down and warms up the rest of your house. And if it is a ceiling-mounted fan, you can draw in the cooler air later in the day at the same time that the hot air is being exhausted. In this case, you would want to wait until twilight and cooler weather, before turning on the fan.

Buying a New Air Conditioner

Selecting the right air conditioner is a confusing business, especially if you want one which is just right for your room or house. If you are in the market for a new unit and want to save operating dollars spent on electricity, here are a few pointers.

Every air conditioner has a cooling capacity expressed in BTU's (British Thermal Units). This refers to the amount of heat it can remove in a one-hour period. The larger the unit, the more expensive it is to run. A unit which is too small, however, can't keep the temperature down. If you must cool the whole house, do it with one central unit rather than a series of window units; it's cheaper.

Make sure your window air conditioner has a high EER rating. EER's are listed on each machine. 10 is best; 8-9 is good; 6-7 is passable (York Division of Borg-Warner Corp.).

Energy Efficiency Ratio (EER). A qualified serviceperson can help you figure what size air conditioner to buy. But you can estimate that it takes about 18 BTU's per hour to cool one square foot. Therefore, a 12,000 BTU unit will cool 660 square feet while an 18,000 BTU unit can cool about 1,000 square feet of space. Besides size, air conditioners vary greatly in efficiency. The efficiency rating of a unit is called its EER or Energy Efficiency Ratio. To find the EER on any unit, divide its cooling capacity BTU rating by its wattage as in the following equation:

$$\frac{\text{BTU Rating}}{\text{Wattage}} = \text{Energy Efficiency Ratio (EER)}$$

For example, if an air conditioner is rated at 12,000 BTU and uses 1,800 watts, its EER is 6.6. Another 12,000 BTU unit may use 1,200 watts. Doing the same division, you get an EER for this unit of 10. The higher the EER the more efficient the machine and you, of course, save money. For every hour you use the higher EER air conditioner mentioned above, you will be saving 600 watts an hour. If you use your air conditioner for 1,000 hours during the cooling season, the difference is 600 kilowatt hours. Now, if you pay an average 7¢ per kwh, the difference in cost to you is $42 a season. Units with high EER's may cost somewhat more, but the energy savings to you should more than make up the difference.

Once the proper-size unit with a satisfactory EER has been purchased, proper installation becomes crucial. If your house is old, new wiring might be necessary (see Wiring in Chapter 6). Have a qualified installer or electrician put in your machine. He will make sure the unit is located out of the sun and in an area which can easily be kept free of leaves, grass and weeds.

Compressor for central air conditioning should be located in a shady area where there aren't many leaf droppings (York Division of Borg-Warner Corp.).

Coping with the System You Own

Although there are newer, more energy efficient air conditioning systems available today, there are numerous things you can do to make the one you already own operate more efficiently. Here are some good economical operating hints.

- Don't leave lights on when they aren't necessary. They add a lot of heat to the room being air conditioned.
- Try not to set the system any more than 20 degrees lower than outside temperature.
- Keep lamps and other heat sources away from the thermostat. Even this small amount of heat will cause a false reading on the instrument and cause your system to work overtime.
- Operate the blower fan on a central system almost continuously to help reduce the amount of time the cooling system must operate.

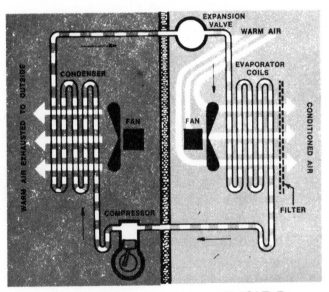

OUTSIDE   INSIDE

Diagram above shows how a typical air conditioner operates.

- Replace all filters prior to and during cooling season to make system run efficiently. (Check directions on your filter; some can be washed, some must be replaced.)
- Do not run attic or window fans when A/C (air conditioning) system is on. If heat builds up in attic, turn the air conditioner off while the fan is removing hot air. Natural static vents will help keep your attic cool while the system is running (see Chapter 4).
- When cooking in the kitchen and air conditioner is on, do turn on exhaust fan to reduce heat buildup. Turn it off as soon as it finishes its task.
- Wash dishes, do laundry, bathe and other such tasks in the early morning before you turn the A/C system on or after you shut it off in the evening. High humidity not only makes the house more uncomfortable in hot weather, but it makes the air conditioning system work longer and harder.
- Always use bathroom exhaust fan after bath to remove heavy moisture buildup.
- Vent dryer outside in summer.
- Place window units on shady and/or north side of house.
- For central air conditioning, make sure outside compressor is not in the sun. Put in fence, trees, etc. to keep in shade.
- Regularly clean diffuser on window and central units.
- Don't block A/C window units with drapes or shades.
- If you use window air conditioning units but have central heating, close the floor or side wall ducts and low return-air grilles. If left open, you will cool area under your house!
- Don't juggle thermostat.
- When going away from home for several days, turn the unit off.
- Eliminate as much of the sun's radiation as possible with the use of shades or blinds.
- Avoid frequent opening and closing of doors when system is on.
- Keep system in top working order by having it checked out just prior to the cooling season or as needed.

4. Ventilation

Ventilation is usually thought of as placement of windows or fans in a home to achieve good air circulation and comfort. But good ventilation, particularly attic ventilation, can contribute to lower energy bills and can prevent major structural damage to your home.

Ventilation has many meanings; to some it means turning on a kitchen fan. But for real energy saving, this chapter considers primarily attic ventilation and how it affects your bills as well as your comfort.

HOW IT HELPS

Unlike many energy-dollar-saving tips described in this book, attic ventilation is not new. In fact, it's very old. A look at 17th century farm houses in the U.S. and Canada may reveal no insulation (unless it was added later) but plenty of attic ventilation. Good attic ventilation was then, and is now, one of the few ways to deal with heat buildup in the summer and moisture buildup in the winter.

Unfortunately attic ventilation has taken a back seat since the invention of insulation and new insulating materials (see Chapter 1). It was thought that since insulation reduced heat transfer, it didn't matter whether or not attic space drastically heated up or grew moist and cold. Time and dollars have proven this theory wrong. We certainly have learned from older, effective attic ventilating systems but we have also increased efficiency through modern techniques. And along with increased efficiency, you can now choose from a variety of systems, many of which you can install yourself.

Does Your Attic Need More Ventilation?

Check the summer heat buildup in your attic. During the hot weather season, you can go up there and feel if it's unusually hot—hotter than any other part of your house. You may wish to place a thermometer there for a 24 hour period and take readings early morning, just before going to bed, and perhaps once during midday. Of course the temperature in your attic should not only be compared to the rest of the house, it should be compared to the temperature outside the house as well. Also ask yourself: Does the temperature cool down in the evening in relation to the temperature outside? Does this condition of an overly hot attic persist throughout the summer?

In a poorly ventilated attic, heat builds up during the day because it is trapped there. Even though the temperature drops at sunset, your attic is not able to release any of this extremely hot air. It simply has nowhere to go, so heat continues to build up day after day; it can easily reach 150 degrees. If you don't use an air conditioner, this means an uncomfortably hot house both day and night. If you do have an air conditioner, it will be working overtime, using a great deal of electric energy. By studying the chart provided, you can specifically see how a properly ventilated attic relieves the situation.

The whole process of an overheated attic starts with heat contacting the roof through the sun's radiation. Heat is transferred in three ways: (1) conduction, transferral through solids; (2) convection, transferral through fluids; and (3) radiation, transferral by electro-magnetic waves. Even on a cloudy day the house is subjected to large amounts of radiation. And anyone who has ever received a severe sunburn at the beach on a cloudy day can testify that the sun's rays are painfully potent.

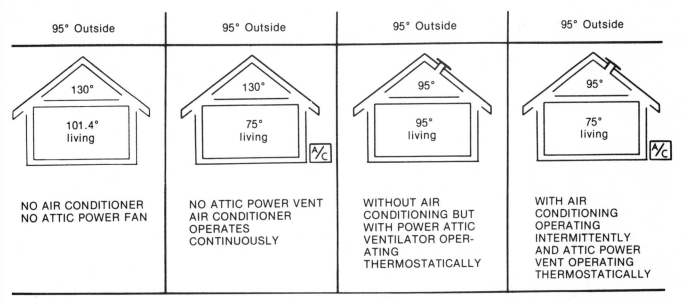

95° Outside	95° Outside	95° Outside	95° Outside
130°	130°	95°	95°
101.4° living	75° living	95° living	75° living
NO AIR CONDITIONER NO ATTIC POWER FAN	NO ATTIC POWER VENT AIR CONDITIONER OPERATES CONTINUOUSLY	WITHOUT AIR CONDITIONING BUT WITH POWER ATTIC VENTILATOR OPERATING THERMOSTATICALLY	WITH AIR CONDITIONING OPERATING INTERMITTENTLY AND ATTIC POWER VENT OPERATING THERMOSTATICALLY

Proper ventilation can greatly reduce the temperature of your superheated attic (Leslie-Locke).

One way you can reduce the amount of radiation hitting your house is by shading techniques (see Chapter 8 on New Room Additions). Another is by using light-colored shingles in order to reflect some of the sun's rays. (You may want to absorb those sun's rays if you have long cold winters, so don't rip off your shingles just yet.) Nevertheless, even light-colored shingles will still absorb most of the sun's rays.

The heat from the shingles and roofing boards is now conducted to the inside surface of the attic space. Here the heated inside surfaces radiate to the attic floor and make it hot. The attic floor or the insulation (in an unfinished attic) acts as a hot plate to heat up the air. And most important, at the same time the attic floor or insulation begins to heat up, it starts to penetrate into the living space below. **Insulation on the attic floor will retard the transfer of heat but it cannot prevent it.**

Adequate ventilation, therefore, is the real key. Not only does it rid the attic space of unwanted heat, it makes the insulation more efficient by reducing the amount of heat with which it has to cope. For you, the hard-pressed homeowner, this can virtually mean shutting off your air conditioner during the night and letting the attic ventilation and open windows cool your home. Or, if you choose to continue to run your air conditioner, it will mean cutting your running and cooling time.

You can also determine whether your attic is properly ventilated during the winter season. Without good ventilation water vapor will penetrate the attic floor insulation and condense in the insulation itself and on the walls and rafters. As described in Chapter 1, once this moisture gets into your insulation, it doesn't work at anywhere near the efficiency of dry insulation. Poor attic ventilation can, therefore, create higher winter heating bills than necessary. You will be spending money for heating all the rooms below your attic, while the warm air is escaping through the wet attic insulation.

There are two circumstances which create water condensation in your attic area during the winter. They are: (1) in cold climates, the combination of high interior humidity—40 percent or greater—and low outside temperatures cause frost to accumulate on the underside of the roof sheathing; (2) in moderate climates with high relative humidity, the day-night temperature cycle combines with high humidity to cause condensation on the underside of the roof.

You will be able to see this moisture condensation (in droplet or in frost form, depending on your climate) in the winter rather than in the summer because almost all of your inside ventilation is closed. (Open windows, screened doors, etc. won't be letting in fresh air or taking out much of the stale, moist air.) Because winter means conserving your heat dollars with a nice tight house and you are trying to avoid drafts or air infiltration, less heat and water vapor escape (from daily use such as cooking, bathing, heating, refrigerator operation, etc). With this tight system and plenty of water vapor, there is only one place for the moisture to go—up into your attic.

So watch for water vapor, frost, or drops in your attic. If you find them, you have ventilation problems. Continually damp structural members such as rafters and beams will deteriorate over time; you could be facing a major repair bill.

TYPES OF ATTIC VENTILATION

If your attic didn't pass the heat buildup or cold-moisture test, you should investigate the two basic types of ventilating systems on the market. One is natural ventilation using static ventilators that require no electricity but depend on the natural wind pressure and thermal effect. The other system is a power ventilator which forces hot air or cold, moist air out of the attic space through electrically powered ventilators. This system, of course, does not depend on the weather conditions, but on electricity. There are a variety of power ventilators, so you may select one which operates on low wattage. You may also want to consider that air conditioners need attic ventilation. So it may pay in some cases to have power ventilators despite the energy cost.

The basic principle of attic ventilation is to change the air and keep it moving so that moisture is removed in the winter and heat in the summer. For summer heat relief, more complete air changes per hour are necessary —about 10 or more times during a one-hour period.

Ventilating equipment, either power or static, must be sized and placed properly to achieve air changes. This air flow is measured in "cubic feet per minute" or CFM. To achieve 10 air changes an hour you need a minimum CFM of 0.7 per square foot of attic area. But tests indicate that maximum attic temperatures are reduced 44.5 percent with a ventilating rate of 1.5 CFM per square foot of attic floor area and 67 percent with 2.0 CFM per square foot. Air changes greater than 2.0 CFM per square foot don't reduce the temperature appreciably.

Static Ventilators

Static ventilators replace the air based on the square footage in your attic in proportion to the area of the clear vent openings. These clear vent openings are reduced somewhat when any sort of obstruction is placed over them. This means grille work, screens, louvered slats, etc. must be taken into consideration and subtracted (usually the manufacturer will do this automatically) when figuring the ratio to square footage in your attic. To strike a balance, use "net free area" of the vent in relation to the floor area (square feet). The ratio is about 150 to 250 square feet to 1 square foot of net free venting. The less square feet of attic space to 1 square foot of net free vent, the faster complete air changes occur.

This should offer an idea of *how many* vents you might need in your attic, but in order to get the maximum air changes per hour, other factors must be considered in static ventilators. The *placement* of the vents is just as crucial for the ultimate result in air change.

The placement of the vents should fully utilize the wind pressure and the thermal effect of your homesite.

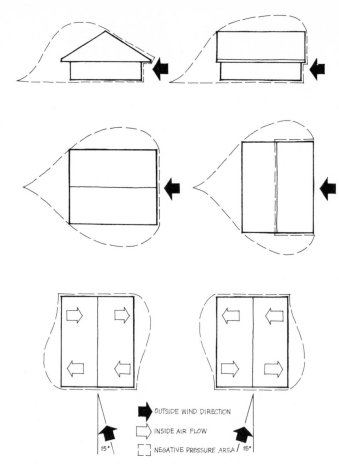

When wind blows against a house, it causes negative and positive pressure areas. Vents in the negative area allow air out, in the positive area they allow air in (H C Products Co.).

Wind pressure is most important. When the wind blows and strikes the side of the roof, it tends to "jump" and thus creates a vacuum or negative pressure on portions of the roof or side of the house. Subsequently this vacuum causes the air to be pulled back toward the house, causing a positive pressure.

Equal quantities of vents must be located within both the positive and negative pressure areas. Vents placed in the negative area will allow the air to be pulled out of the attic; vents placed in the positive area will pull air into the attic.

Placement of vents are also influenced by the thermal effect. Due to the principle that hot air rises, high vents will let out the escaping overheated air while low vents will replace the hot air with the cooler outside air.

Because there is no guarantee that wind pressure and thermal effect will continually change the air, other considerations come into play. Static ventilators must take into account changes in wind direction, therefore vents are placed as "continuously" as possible. This will minimize the difference in wind direction by allowing the net free area to be effective regardless of wind direction.

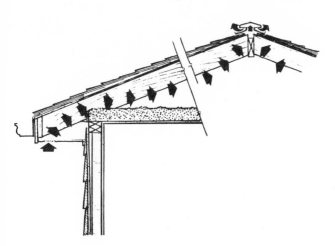

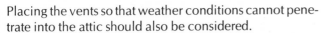

As hot air rises out of the top vents, cooler air replaces it in the lower vents. Good ventilation always takes advantage of this thermal effect (H C Products Co.).

Placing the vents so that weather conditions cannot penetrate into the attic should also be considered.

The initial cost of static ventilators is not high. Small end vents can run you as little as $4 or $5 per vent. Larger continuous vents cost about $2 to $5 a running foot. Labor costs can vary drastically. The more extensive your roof cutting (to place vents), the higher your labor charges. The air-change efficiency offered by this system is good, and there are a number of combinations of vents available. It is not a difficult job for a do-it-yourselfer who wants to tackle it. But he or she must be willing to spend the time.

The following illustrations show the different types of static attic vents. They cannot and should not be used alone, but only in combination with each other. The combinations and how they work are also illustrated.

Roof louvers. These small domes are mounted near the ridge of the roof. Aluminum ones are the least expensive; plastic, steel or wood are priced higher. Available with screen or slit openings to prevent insect penetration. Screens may cut down on airflow and get clogged with dust, dirt or insects. Slit-type designs resist insect penetration and avoid clogging problems.

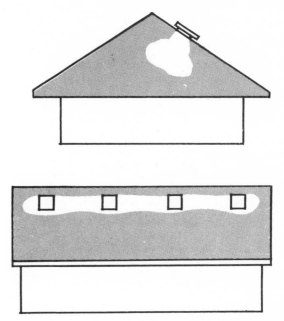

Only a small area between roof louvers is affected by the vent (H C Products Co.).

Turbine wheel. This can be thought of as a variation on the roof louver. The difference is that the turbine wheel turns when there is sufficient wind and so it can draw air out of the attic space more effectively. Both turbine wheel and roof louvers vent only the area between the louvers and severe weather conditions may penetrate through them. They can be purchased in sizes from 40 square inches to 80 square inches of net free area.

Gable-end louvers. Usually triangular (rectangular ones also available), they are mounted in the top point of the two gables. When the wind is perpendicular to the

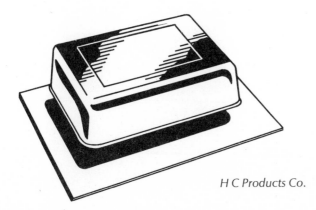

H C Products Co.

H C Products Co.

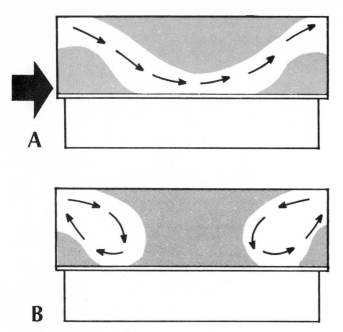

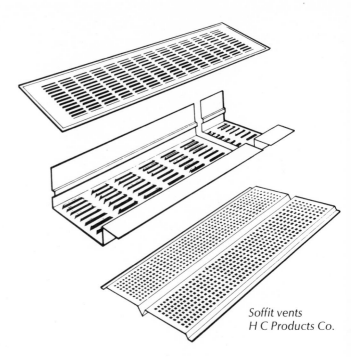

Soffit vents
H C Products Co.

(A) The effect of parallel winds on gable-end louvers; (B) Perpendicular wind effect on same louvers (H C Products Co.).

vents, the same vent acts as both an intake and exhaust. The air change is small. When the wind is blowing parallel to the gable ends, one louver acts as an intake and the other as an exhaust. In this manner the rate of flow of air into the attic is equivalent to 70 percent of the wind velocity. As the air enters, it moves toward the floor and then up and out the other vent. The area of air flow, however, is limited in width by the size of the vent. It also permits severe weather conditions to penetrate. The units come in various sizes from less than 40 square inches to several hundred square inches of net free area.

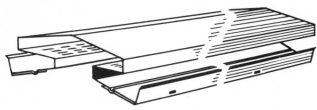

H C Products Co.

Ridge vents. This type of vent provides a continuous opening along the entire ridge line of the roof. Mainly available in aluminum in 10-foot lineal sections or in 4-foot self-contained units. You can figure the net free area is 18 square inches per lineal foot. Primarily an exhaust vent, it provides uniform continuous air flow along the entire roof sheath surface.

Soffit vents. This type of vent offers the only air flow which is near the floor plus effective air circulation no matter what the wind direction. This occurs because the

vents are positioned on the horizontal and therefore are always parallel to the wind. But don't plan on this type of vent drastically reducing floor temperatures during the summer. It's that radiation problem again, and unfortunately the roof sheathing is not cooled by this venting system.

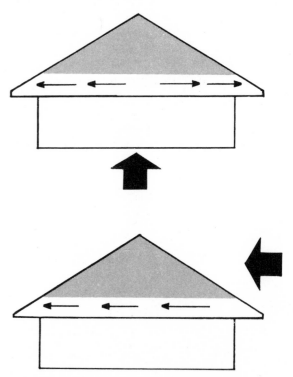

Soffit vents are effective regardless of wind direction but do little to lower attic floor temperature (H C Products Co.).

Vent Combinations

As you can see by the illustrations, no one type of vent will really work for all the problems of natural ventilation such as: (1) wind pressure; (2) thermal effect; (3) radiation heat; (4) wind direction; (5) weather conditions.

The roof louvers, even large numbers of them, will not give proper ventilation if used alone because the only area vented is between the various roof louvers. Also, unusual weather conditions can force moisture into the attic space which cannot be removed later.

Gable-end louvers offer ventilation of a small area and do not achieve maximum efficiency with perpendicular winds. Like the roof louver, moisture can be forced into the attic when this type of venting is used alone.

Ridge vents are always in the negative pressure area and that is why they become an effective exhaust. But if this vent were installed alone, it would have to serve as both an inlet and exhaust vent and would confine air flow to the top of the attic near the ridge.

Soffit vents take care of wind direction and air movement but cannot deal effectively with radiation heat buildup.

Since ridge vents, gable-end louvers and roof louvers are used in a similar manner and physically they are placed high, they each combine well with soffit vents, which have low and continuous placement in the attic.

Roof louvers with soffit vents. Although this combination provides high and low vent areas, it is practically impossible to install enough high vent area for a balanced system. The combination provides about the same amount (not type) of ventilation per square inch of vent area as soffit vents alone. Air movement is confined to a few areas adjacent to roof and floor.

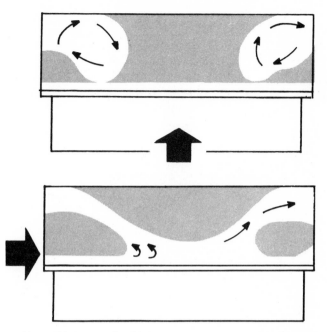

Gable-end louver and soffit-vent system does not alter air flow patterns of each unit (H C Products Co.).

Gable-end louvers with soffit vents. Again a combination of high and low vents. The combination leaves the air flow patterns the same as when each type of vent is used alone. This means that most of the air movement is adjacent to the attic floor.

Ridge vents and soffit vents. This combination utilizes the highest vent and the lowest vent and offers an efficient system to make the most of the thermal effect, wind pressure and direction. The continuous soffit vent supplies the attic with enough air to assure a steady flow out through the ridge vent along the entire roof sheath surface.

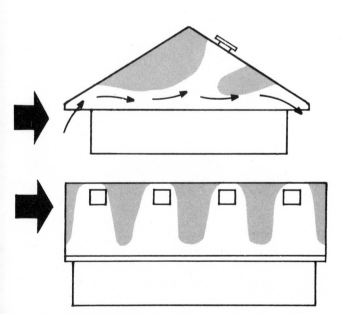

It is difficult to balance the air flow with a roof louver and soffit vent system (H C Products Co.).

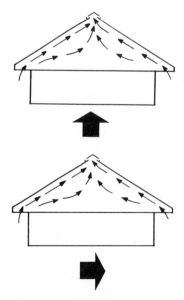

Ridge and soffit vents provide the best combination (H C Products Co.).

NET FREE AREA (SQ. IN.) TO VENTILATE ATTIC

	Width (in feet)															
	20	22	24	26	28	30	32	34	36	38	40	42	44	46	48	50
20	192	211	230	250	269	288	307	326	346	365	384	403	422	441	461	480
22	211	232	253	275	296	317	338	359	380	401	422	444	465	485	506	528
24	230	253	276	300	323	346	369	392	415	438	461	484	507	530	553	576
26	250	275	300	324	349	374	399	424	449	474	499	524	549	574	599	624
28	269	296	323	349	376	403	430	457	484	511	538	564	591	618	645	662
30	288	317	346	374	403	432	461	490	518	547	576	605	634	662	691	720
32	307	338	369	399	430	461	492	522	553	584	614	645	675	706	737	768
34	326	359	392	424	457	490	522	555	588	620	653	685	717	750	782	815
36	346	380	415	449	484	518	553	588	622	657	691	726	760	795	829	864
38	365	401	438	474	511	547	584	620	657	693	730	766	803	839	876	912
40	384	422	461	499	538	576	614	653	691	730	768	806	845	883	922	960
42	403	444	484	524	564	605	645	685	726	766	806	847	887	927	968	1008
44	422	465	507	549	591	634	676	718	760	803	845	887	929	971	1013	1056
46	442	486	530	574	618	662	707	751	795	839	883	927	972	1016	1060	1104
48	461	507	553	599	645	691	737	783	829	876	922	968	1014	1060	1106	1152
50	480	528	576	624	672	720	768	816	864	912	960	1008	1056	1104	1152	1200
52	499	549	599	649	699	749	799	848	898	948	998	1048	1098	1148	1198	1248
54	518	570	622	674	726	778	830	881	933	985	1037	1089	1141	1192	1244	1296
56	538	591	645	699	753	807	860	914	967	1021	1075	1130	1184	1237	1291	1345
58	557	612	668	724	780	835	891	946	1002	1058	1113	1170	1226	1282	1337	1392
60	576	634	691	749	807	864	922	979	1037	1094	1152	1210	1267	1324	1382	1440
62	595	655	714	774	834	893	953	1012	1071	1131	1190	1250	1309	1369	1428	1488
64	614	676	737	799	861	922	983	1045	1106	1168	1229	1291	1352	1413	1475	1536
66	634	697	760	824	888	950	1014	1077	1140	1204	1268	1331	1394	1458	1522	1585
68	653	718	783	849	914	979	1045	1110	1175	1240	1306	1371	1436	1501	1567	1632
70	672	739	806	874	941	1008	1075	1142	1210	1276	1344	1411	1478	1545	1613	1680

(Length in feet — vertical column)

FHA Chart   Chart utilizes 1/300 ratio; double for 1/150 ratio; divide by five for 1/1500 ratio.

Chart gives the amount of net free area (in square inches) required to ventilate attic space of home. To use chart, measure length and width of each rectangular section of your attic. Locate length dimensions on the vertical column and width dimensions on the horizontal column.

For the do-it-yourselfer interested in undertaking this project, use the chart to estimate the amount of venting you will need for your attic space (in inches of net free area). Remember the ratio of 1 to 150 is considered good; the ratio of 1 to 300 is considered absolute minimum. Most homes usually have some sort of eave or soffit venting in them.

Power Ventilators

Power vents run on electricity, and are often used in homes where no ventilating system has been installed. Less venting holes have to be cut into the roof or eaves with this system, so that easy installation and effective ventilation are achieved quickly.

Power ventilators are usually equipped with a thermostat which activates the unit at a preselected temperature and shuts it off when the temperature is sufficiently reduced. Some work off a manual switch; most simply plug into an electric socket. The vents are located on the rear slope of the roof, near the peak and centered. Air intakes are located at the eaves. This combination reaches all attic space sufficiently. Power gable vents are available if roofing vents are unsatisfactory.

Typical roof power ventilator (Kool-o-matic).

POWER VENTILATOR REQUIREMENTS

								WIDTH IN FEET								
	20	**22**	**24**	**26**	**28**	**30**	**32**	**34**	**36**	**38**	**40**	**42**	**44**	**46**	**48**	**50**
20	280	308	336	364	392	420	448	476	504	532	560	588	616	644	672	700
22	308	339	370	400	431	462	493	524	554	585	616	647	678	708	739	770
24	336	370	403	437	470	504	538	571	605	638	672	706	739	773	806	840
26	364	400	437	473	510	546	582	619	655	692	728	764	801	837	874	910
28	392	431	470	510	549	588	627	666	706	745	784	823	862	902	941	980
30	420	462	504	546	588	630	672	714	756	798	840	882	924	966	1008	1050
32	448	493	538	582	627	672	717	761	806	851	896	941	986	1030	1075	1120
34	476	524	571	619	666	714	762	809	857	904	952	1000	1047	1095	1142	1190
36	504	554	604	655	706	756	806	857	907	958	1008	1058	1109	1159	1210	1260
38	532	585	638	692	745	798	851	904	958	1011	1064	1117	1170	1224	1277	1330
40	560	616	672	728	784	840	896	952	1008	1064	1120	1176	1232	1288	1344	1400
42	588	647	706	764	823	882	941	1000	1058	1117	1176	1234	1294	1352	1411	1470
44	616	678	739	801	862	924	986	1047	1109	1170	1232	1294	1355	1417	1478	1540
46	644	708	773	837	902	966	1030	1095	1159	1224	1288	1352	1417	1481	1546	1610
48	672	739	806	874	941	1008	1075	1142	1210	1277	1344	1411	1478	1546	1613	1680
50	700	770	840	910	980	1050	1120	1190	1260	1330	1400	1470	1540	1610	1680	1750
52	728	801	874	946	1019	1092	1165	1238	1310	1383	1456	1529	1602	1674	1747	1820
54	756	832	907	983	1058	1134	1210	1285	1361	1436	1512	1588	1663	1739	1814	1890
56	784	862	941	1019	1098	1176	1254	1333	1411	1490	1568	1646	1725	1803	1882	1960
58	812	893	974	1056	1137	1218	1299	1380	1462	1543	1624	1705	1786	1868	1949	2030
60	840	924	1008	1092	1176	1260	1344	1428	1512	1596	1680	1764	1848	1932	2016	2100
62	868	955	1042	1128	1215	1302	1389	1476	1562	1649	1736	1823	1910	1996	2083	2170
64	896	986	1075	1165	1254	1344	1434	1523	1613	1702	1792	1882	1971	2061	2150	2240
66	924	1016	1108	1201	1294	1386	1478	1571	1663	1756	1848	1940	2033	2125	2218	2310
68	952	1047	1142	1238	1333	1428	1523	1618	1714	1809	1904	1999	2094	2190	2285	2380
70	980	1078	1176	1274	1372	1470	1568	1666	1764	1862	1960	2058	2156	2254	2352	2450

(LENGTH IN FEET — left vertical axis)

HVI Chart

To determine what size power ventilator is needed to cool your attic efficiently, find the length of your attic on the vertical column and the width on the horizontal column. Where two columns intersect, you will find the required CFM rated ventilator (Courtesy of Home Ventilating Institute).

Louvered-end power ventilator (NuTone Division of Scovill).

Estimate the size of the power vent needed for your attic based on achieving at least 10 complete air changes per hour. The chart shown gives you specifications based on your attic area. Wattage of the power vents will, of course, vary. There are some on the market that operate on 75 watts. When you purchase one, make sure you buy the lowest wattage ventilator that still delivers the highest efficiency CFM. Ask the salesperson for the machine's EER rating. (See Chapter 3 for EER details.)

For those who are installing power ventilators themselves, use these illustrations as a guide. Keep in mind that most homes usually have static vents in the eaves.

Attic power ventilators are not difficult to install. Although manufacturer's specification sheet should always be followed, the four basic steps include (left to right) cutting hole in roof, fit- *ting unit into hole from outside, tightening unit down, and adding outside cap to prevent weather infiltration (Leigh Prod. Inc.).*

SPECIFIC AREA VENTILATION

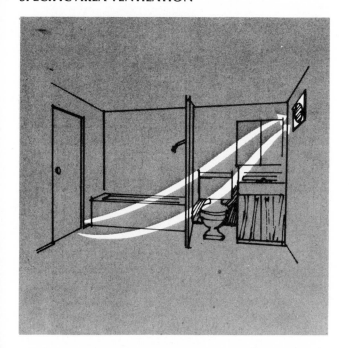

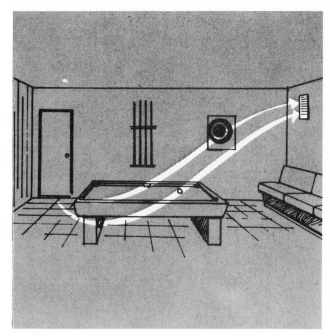

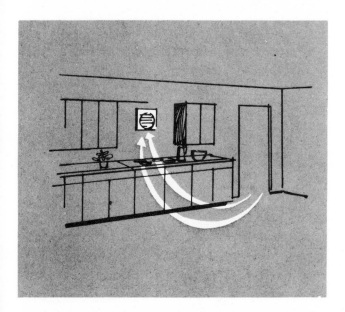

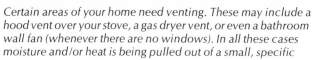

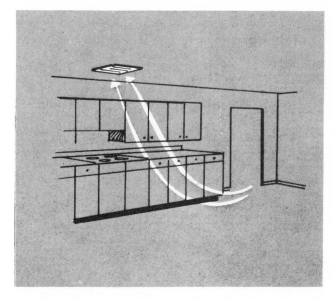

Certain areas of your home need venting. These may include a hood vent over your stove, a gas dryer vent, or even a bathroom wall fan (whenever there are no windows). In all these cases moisture and/or heat is being pulled out of a small, specific area. This will reduce the load on an air conditioner or simply increase your family's comfort level (courtesy of the Home Ventilating Institute).

With the variety of lights available many different effects can be achieved economically. (A) With all lighting systems on full, this room is well lighted but without glare. Downlights over fireplace are low wattage incandescent lamps, while paneling is lighted with warm white fluorescents behind cornice board. Recessed in the ceiling are low wattage incandescent spotlights.

All can be dimmer controlled. Table lamp is on a three-way switch. (B) Brick wall is highlighted by ceiling spots while other lights are dimmed. (C) With just a 75-watt spotlight over flowers on table, and two more directly over front of chairs, room is conversationally lighted yet visually enlarged (General Electric Company).

5. Lighting

Of all the home energy wastes, lighting is probably one of the simplest to spot. The visual energy output at your house could probably be reduced quite easily; with a bit of planning, both the esthetic and practical needs of your family can be improved. Even though this area of conservation won't save the largest amount of dollars, it will help without causing discomfort.

With today's varied lighting market—strip lighting, spot lighting, lanterns and lights on pivots, lights built into furniture or stair rails, recessed into ceilings or walls or on baseboards, fluorescent and incandescent or even newer types on the market—a good-looking and efficient lighting arrangement can be achieved. Many items can be purchased from lighting-fixture stores or can be made-to-order by the homeowner as a do-it-yourself project. In any event, the purpose is threefold:

(1) to lower your lighting bill and conserve electric energy;

(2) to come up with better lighting for the money spent; and

(3) to achieve a smart-looking room using the latest and most efficient lighting effects.

Some general questions that often confuse the homeowner are: Should you plan an overhead lighting fixture? Will spot lighting certain areas of the room be more economical than general room lights? How much light will your family need to feel comfortable watching television, doing a jigsaw puzzle, studying, crocheting mittens, playing Monopoly? Are lights over the stove or sink a good idea? Do light-colored rooms actually save on electricity? Do fluorescent lights really offer the same amount of light at half the cost? What exactly are lumens? Soft light bulbs? Are there any new incandescent bulbs on the market which save on energy output? Should you install a light dimmer as a do-it-yourself project or is it just a fancy "extra" used in high-priced homes? These questions can be answered and should be, for the homeowner who seriously wants to cut light bills.

Figuring Costs

All electrical costs are figured on a per kilowatt hour basis (called kwh). That is if a 100-watt bulb is burned for 10 hours, you have consumed 10 hours times 100 watts (100 x 10 = 1,000) or 1,000 watts which equals one kilowatt hour. The amount of energy that is used at your home is registered on the electric meter usually located in the basement or on the outside of your house. Naturally the meter is constantly changing, and it is read usually monthly or bi-monthly. The difference on the meter readings is subtracted—the older month's reading is subtracted from the newer reading—and that is the amount of kwh consumed by your family over that period. You can read the meter yourself and do a quick check on how much electricity you've used.

Knowing these figures may help you come up with a rough idea of how much each kwh costs. Many electric companies bill the homeowner on a sliding scale. The first 30 kwh may cost you $5 while the next 200 will cost somewhat less. Then again, some companies have special rates for families who use "off-peak" hours of electricity (see Chapter 6 about off-peak hours) and most have

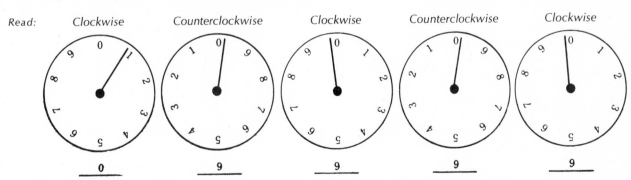

Reading an electric meter is similar to telling time. There are either four or five "clocks" to read with numbers that are arranged differently. Dials should be read from right to left and the numbers written down in the same order. If the needle on the dial is between numbers, record the smaller. This meter reads 99990. The older reading on your meter is subtracted from the latest one for the number of kwh used during that period (Portland General Electric Co.).

summer and winter rates. Nevertheless, even a rough estimate of what each average kwh costs can be extremely helpful in cutting down on your bills.

Here's how. Look at your electric bill and divide the amount of dollars charged for electricity by the amount of kwh used. If you're charged $50 for 700 kwh, you divide $50 by 700 and come up with .07 or 7¢ per kwh. This is probably a somewhat high rate but electricity per kwh can be found from 2¢ to 10¢. That's quite a spread, but different outputs for different areas influence electricity costs.

According to estimates, the average family of four uses 1,200 to 2,400 kwh monthly. This figure can and will vary according to each family's size and lifestyle, as well as whether or not such items as electric heat, hot water, stoves, etc. are included on the electric budget. If you wish, you can read your meter one month and compare your use of kwh to the "average." You can however, figure that burning a 100-watt bulb for 10 hours on the exterior of your house each night means you consume 1 kwh daily. Over the period of a year you consume 365 kwh for that light. If you replace it with a 50-watt bulb, you could cut your wattage and so your energy output in half. This saves half the money or about $12.77 each year on just one light. By multiplying this type of savings throughout your house, you can add up dollar savings quickly.

Bulb Snatching

Unfortunately most people think that by reducing the wattage on a bulb, they must automatically reduce the amount of light it gives. That often is not the case at all. A watt is simply the amount of electricity consumed by the bulb. *Lumens* are the real measure of the amount of brightness or light emitted by the bulbs. And bulb life tells approximately how long the bulb will last before burning out. All this information is necessary for the wise consumer to have at his/her fingertips, and manufacturers must label these facts on each bulb package. You can now compare the amount of light you're getting (lumens) for the amount of energy it will cost you (watts).

As a consumer you should look carefully at long-life bulbs. You will see that these bulbs only furnish about 80 percent of the lumens for the same wattage. It then becomes a trade-off between more light for the money or more bulb-life money expended on electricity. (You may wish to consider these long-lasting bulbs for hard-to-reach places such as high hall lights or post lanterns, etc.)

The key to making these decisions is based on knowing how many lumens are necessary for different activities in your home—TV watching, knitting, reading, walking up stairways or in halls, washing dishes or using the workshop down in your basement. The accompanying chart tells you how many lumens are necessary for each task listed.

Again, buyer beware! Although one 150-watt bulb offers 2,880 lumens, two 75-watt bulbs (equal energy output) only offer 2,380 lumens. Remember that larger wattage bulbs are generally more efficient and produce more lumens per watt than smaller bulbs. It generally requires six 25-watt bulbs to give the same amount of light as only one 100-watt bulb.

The buyer should also be aware that different types of lights can offer lower wattage for higher amounts of lumens and throw in for good measure a longer-lasting life.

To save on your electric light bill you should thoroughly understand the relationships between watts and lumens, your options on various light sources, and the

Specific Visual Task	Lumens
Reading and writing: handwriting,	
indistinct print, or poor copies	70
Books, magazines, newspapers	30
Music scores, advanced	70
Music scores, simple	30
Studying at desk	70
Recreation:	
Playing cards, billiards	30
Table tennis	20
Grooming:	
Shaving, combing hair, applying makeup	50
Kitchen work:	
At sink	70
At range	50
At work counters	50
Laundering jobs:	
At washer	50
At ironing board	50
At ironer	50
Sewing:	
Dark fabrics (fine detail, low contrast)	200
Prolonged periods (light to medium fabrics)	100
Occasional (light-colored fabrics)	50
Occasional (coarse thread, large stitched,	
high contrast of thread to fabric)	30
Handicraft:	
Close work (reading diagrams and	
blueprints, fine finishing)	100
Cabinet making, planing, sanding, glueing	50
Measuring, sawing, assembling, repairing	50
Any area involving a visual task	30
For safety in passage areas	10
Areas used mostly for relaxation,	
recreation and conversation	10

amount of lumens needed for certain activity areas of your home. You should then decide if certain areas in your house have been overlighted and can now be cut down both in wattage and in lumens. Or you may realize that you need more lumens. Don't automatically assume you still can't cut the cost. You can.

Because there are basically three types of light bulbs that can now be bought today, the consumer does have options on electric-light savings. The basic bulbs are fluorescent, high intensity discharge (HID) and incandescent. Unfortunately these types of lights cannot be interchanged by simply screwing in the different bulbs. Changing the light fixture is usually necessary. But in many cases you can and should switch to save electric costs.

Fluorescent lighting. Most households use fluorescent lights to a certain extent. They are probably the cheapest source of lumens available for the money. These bulbs use 75 percent less energy than a comparable popular incandescent bulb. You can get the same amount of light from a 25-watt fluorescent light bulb as you can from a 100-watt incandescent. Fluorescent lights also deliver about 10 to 25 times the life expectancy as that of an incandescent bulb. These bulbs come in narrow tube strips 1½ inches in diameter about 12 inches long to 4 feet long. Or they are shaped into circles ranging in size from 6 inches to 24 inches in diamater. They may cost more than incandescent, but pay for themselves in the long run.

Fluorescent lights are very good energy savers, giving more light for less energy. Warm white bulbs offer the best light and shadow. Either in tubes or in circles, fluorescents serve many purposes. The spiral one above can also be used as an inside "grow" light above your favorite plants (Duro-Lite Lamps, Inc.).

Energy comparison for incandescent bulbs and fluorescent tubes			
	Incandescent bulb	Deluxe fluorescent tube	Fluorescent Advantages
Watts	75	30 (44 total input watts)	31-watt (or 41 percent) energy saving
Bulb life	750 hours	15,000 hours	lasts 14,250 hours more (or 20 times longer)
Light emitted	1180 lumens	1530 lumens	350 more lumens, or 30 percent more light

Lumen outputs of standard and long-life incandescent bulbs				
	Watts	Lumens	Bulb life (hrs)	Lumens/watt
Standard bulbs	100	1740	750	17.4
	75	1180	750	15.7
Long-life bulbs	100	1690	1150	16.9
	100	1490	2500	14.9
	100	1470	3000	14.7
	92	1490	2500	16.2
	90	1290	3500	14.3

The great disadvantage of fluorescent lighting lies in the quality of light they deliver. The light seems to flicker and often the shade of light can make people or things look "sickly" or peculiarly colored. This type of light has a completely different shadow effect than is considered normal. Something is being done to rectify these problems. Now you can purchase fluorescent bulbs in several tones which have been color-corrected, such as warm white. (Another new fluorescent light is becoming available—one that fits into an incandescent socket. Be on the lookout for it.) You may want to use fluorescent lighting for valance lights, wall bracket units, luminous ceilings and countertop lighting.

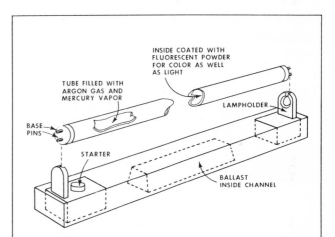

The fluorescent phosphor coating on the inside of the tube is activated by electric energy passing through the tube; light is given off. The starter in standard starter-type fixtures permits preheating of the electrodes in the ends of the tube to make it easier to start. The ballast limits the current to keep the tube functioning properly. The channel holds ballast and wiring and spaces the lampholders.

(Dept. of Agriculture).

High intensity discharge lighting (HID). Another way to cut light bills is to use mercury and metal halide lamps for highly efficient lighting. These units can give from 2 to 5 times as much light as an incandescent bulb for the same amount of watts. These are small lamp fixtures directing high intensity beams of light on a small area. Good for task and area lighting, especially outside. The HID lights are easy to maintain—they last 10 to 30 times longer than similar incandescent bulbs. They come in colors and tones similar to incandescents.

Incandescent lighting. This is the oldest bulb in use—80 years in the American household and now there is a distinct variation on this type of bulb, crypton gas bulbs. These bulbs are interchangeable with incandescent bulbs in any one of your present light sockets. They are more expensive to purchase than regular incandescent bulbs but have a longer-lasting life without losing any lumens. They also save on wattage.

This incandescent light, which uses 8 percent less energy and gives the same amount of light as an ordinary bulb, is filled with crypton gas (Duro-Lite Lamps Inc.).

Regular incandescent bulbs that have long been on the market now come in three modest variations such as inside-frost, inside-white (silica-coated which is the most common) and clear. These bulbs come in a variety of shapes from tiny teardrops to huge spot lights and of course can be purchased in virtually every supermarket across the country.

Although this most popular and common household bulb is the most expensive one to use, incandescent lamps are considered the smallest and most versatile for the home. Incandescent lighting also permits close control. If you choose to use incandescent lights, here are two key ways to conserve your electric output and lower your light bill: (1) use a three-way light bulb wherever possible, and (2) install dimmer switches. Both suggestions work on the same principle. By using lower or dimmer lights whenever possible, you use less watts and therefore less energy; the lower cost is reflected immediately in your light bill.

A *three-way bulb* is made so that you can get three different watts and lumen intensities. The three-way bulb is the most economical of the incandescents because the wattage can be controlled very easily. You simply install a three-way bulb in a socket that is geared for it and the switch turns to three different light intensities (50-100-150) always starting from the lowest to the highest. If your light needs are satisfied by one of the earlier intensities, you can stop there! The three-way bulbs often avoid the expense of installing other fixtures around that area which may need higher or lower lighting. Any multi-purpose light fixture will eventually save you money.

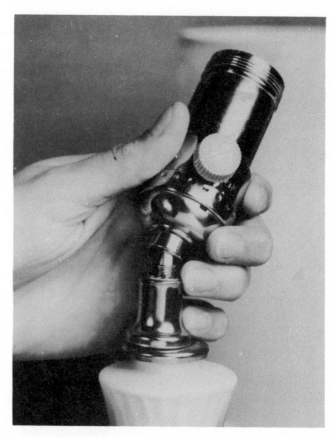

You can replace the socket on any lamp for a full-range dimmer using only a screwdriver (Leviton Manufacturing Co.).

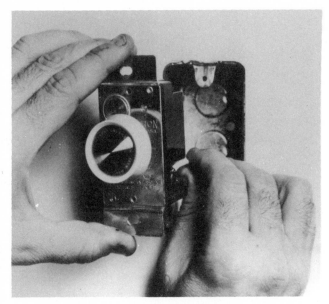

After shutting off electric power, wall dimmers can be installed with a screwdriver. Take off your old wall switch to expose the two wires. Insert new dimmer switch and attach and wrap wires as directed on your instructions. Refasten switch plate (Leviton Manufacturing Co.).

The *dimmer* can be installed in the wall or attached to light cords. It has numerous settings, from off to full-bright. Units are easily installed. See the following illustrations for exact instructions on how to put them in. Although the dimmer costs about $5 to $10, the switch can almost pay for itself in a year if used regularly. It certainly allows you to set the mood and save money and energy at the same time.

Future Lighting. In less than two years, you may be able to purchase a new type of light which will last for 10 years and save energy at the same time. Instead of producing illumination with the glowing tungsten filament found in incandescent bulbs, it uses a cool magnet coil which energizes mercury vapor in the bulb.

PLANNING BRIGHT IDEAS

Even though your home may be completely "lit up," with a little bit of pushing and pulling, you can whack off dollars from your light bill. First take a couple of minutes and make a fast sketch of your home noting activities conducted in each room and area within the room. Jot down colors, decorative themes, where windows are located, and other natural light sources in the room.

The next step is to look at your sketch and see if your light is too strong or too weak by comparing it to the chart of lumens-to-tasks. The brighter lights and high intensities will be used for more detailed eye work such as reading,

Bright lights and high intensities are needed for the more detailed work done in your tool room (Progress Lighting).

sewing, or working in the tool room. Less lumens will be needed for TV-watching (make sure that one light is on) or in hallways. But the rooms should all be free of glare or unevenly distributed light, which causes eye strain as eyes travel from deep shadows to highly lighted areas. Hallways should have a light fixture about every 8 feet, while general lighting should cover 40 or 50 square feet (if fluorescent light is used, it should cover 100 square feet). You can keep your general lighting at low intensity if you use area lights over your stove, kitchen sink, on desks, etc. Overhead fixtures are useful in dining rooms but are not always necessary in bedrooms.

The first way to cut down on your light bill is to take advantage of the cheapest source of light—the sun. It might pay to simply rearrange your room to have a desk near a window that gets the sun (without drafts during the cold weather), or place a sewing machine near a window so sunlight hits over your left shoulder. This might apply for any form of close eye work done during the daylight hours. Not only will you avoid paying additional light costs but your family may avoid eye-strain during the day when they might need extra illumination but feel foolish turning on a lamp.

You can keep your general lighting at low intensity if you utilize area lights over your stove, kitchen sink, and similar areas (NuTone).

Skylights offer the same sort of electric light savings. If you have them in your home, make sure you take full advantage of them.

Another way to save light energy is to use the decor of your room so that you make the fullest use of all your light sources, both natural and electrical. Light-colored

wall, ceilings and bright wall paper will capture and reflect the light so that less lumens are required. Light-colored ceilings reflect the light downward and provide better lighting efficiency. (Make sure your lamps take advantage of this and reflect light upward as well as down—there is less glare and shadow, also.)

This type of thinking can go a long way to save money when it's time to redecorate the darker rooms in your house, such as a finished basement or attic. You may find that you want to push up your painting and papering ahead of your usual schedule if there is a decided dark and gloomy quality to those rooms, which seem to require lights at all times. For those who have lovely dark wood interiors which present the same problem but not, obviously, the same solution, you could consider ''pickling'' the wood. This is a process of white-washing the wood quickly and wiping it off. (Try it on a small piece of wood from a lumber yard with the same finish as your interior.) It lightens the wood without losing all the tones and grain pattern. But there will be a decided change in the appearance of your room; those who like dark wood will probably not be happy.

Next you may want to consider a couple of simple lighting renovations. You can install track lighting in

One of the newest and most versatile types of lights is track lighting. Here the ceiling fixture highlights sculpture and panelling (Halo Lighting).

Track lights can be swiveled so that intense beams are directed to specific areas. Here track lighting shines down on piano music and paintings. The absence of deep shadows prevents glare (Halo Lighting).

Light-colored walls, ceilings, and bright wallpaper, will capture and reflect light so that less lumens are required (Window Shade Manufacturers Assn.).

A

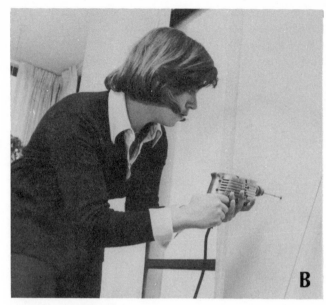

B

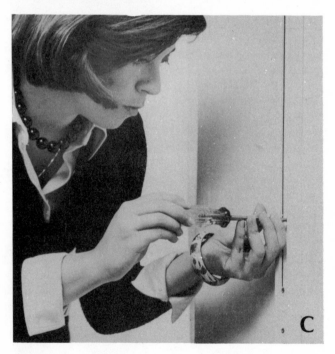

C

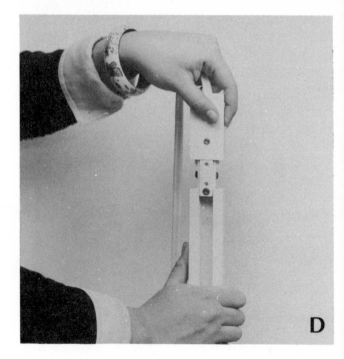

D

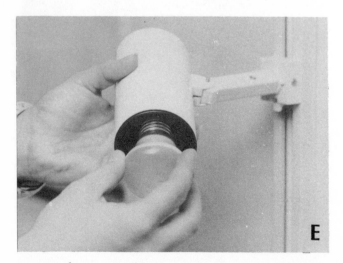

E

Install track lighting in five steps. (A) Place track on wall and mark fastening positions. (B) Drill holes. (C) Fasten track to wall with screws from kit. (D) Insert cord and plug connecter. (E) Once lamps are placed in the track, insert bulbs. (Halo Lighting).

order to direct the light precisely where you want it, without wasting lumens. These units consist of slim electrified metal strips set flush on the wall or even recessed. Spot lights, either squares, cylinders, or spheres, are clipped onto the strip anywhere, without using tools. The light beam is then positioned and swiveled to direct light wherever needed—a wall painting, shelves of books or sculptures.

Follow the instructions given to install track lighting yourself.

How to Buy Lights

You may want to purchase some of the new lamps or fixtures now on the market. In selecting lamps, keep in mind that for maximum use of light the table height plus the lamp base height to the lower edge of the shade, should equal the eye-height of the person using the lamp. The same applies to floor lamps. And lamp shades with white material are preferable since they help reflect the light. They should be large enough to conceal the light bulb to reduce glare.

You can estimate that the bottom of a lamp shade should be about 40 to 42 inches from the floor; that's the average level. Usually a 16-inch diameter is the smallest lamp shade recommended for reading.

Light-Saving Tips

Here are a number of inexpensive and fast energy-saving tips which you can use in your home to cut overall energy consumption. Some may be obvious to efficient home managers but others are less practiced.

- In closets that have a light, install an automatic switch that shuts off the light when the door is closed, and of course keep the closet door closed when not in use. (Closed closets save heat money, too.)
- Use a wise hand with outdoor lights. Turn them off after company arrives and on again as your company leaves—off when they're gone. And don't switch on outside lights during the time you're absent from the house. Many would-be burglars look for this as a sign that no one is home.
- When lights are required outdoors for security, a photoelectric cell which turn lights off automatically at dawn and back on at dusk is a wise investment.

- Turn off incandescent lights whenever you leave a room, even for a few minutes. There is no surge of power when you turn them on again.
- Don't turn off fluorescent lights if you leave the room for less than 15 minutes. This type of lighting does use more electricity when it's being turned off and on, and this shortens the life of the bulb.
- HID lights should be turned off just as with incandescent.
- Use three-way bulbs and dimmer units wherever possible.
- In rooms such as basements or garages which are not used regularly and cannot be checked quickly to see if lights are burning, you can install a switch with a red pilot or indicator on it. If the red light shines it means there's a light on in that room. You can purchase these switches at all hardware stores.
- Dust all light fixtures regularly. A bulb coated with dust causes family members to turn on more lights than necessary for the job.
- Know the right light for your needs. Buy bulbs carefully, reading all information on lumens, watts and long life.
- Put bright new bulbs where you need the most light and put the old darker bulbs in areas such as basements or garages.
- Use the smallest wattage bulbs acceptable for casual lighting and where specific usage and safety will not be impaired.
- Arrange your rooms to take advantage of all the sunlight possible. Keep shades up in the winter during daylight.
- Use lights over specific areas such as stove and sink whenever possible and turn off immediately when finished.
- Keep rooms free of glare and extreme contrasts of deep shadows and brightly lit areas. Beware of lights shining directly on shiny surfaces such as your TV screen.
- Use fluorescent and HID lights whenever possible.
- Buy lamps and fixtures with an eye to reflective qualities as well as good looks.
- Don't leave lights burning in parts of your house whenever you are on vacation to keep burglars away. Invest in clock timers which turn lights on at dusk and off again at bedtime to make your home seem really occupied.

check	appliance and typical wattage	average use	average monthly kilowatt-hour use	your average cost per kilowatt-hour	estimated monthly cost
	air conditioning**				
___	window unit 9000 Btu/hr	8 hours per day	321 kwh	X ___	= ___
___	central system 24,000 Btu/hr	8 hours per day	857 kwh	X ___	= ___
___	**baby food warmer** 165 watts	3 times per day	3 kwh	X ___	= ___
___	**blanket*** 150 watts	every night	19 kwh	X ___	= ___
___	**blender** 385 watts	6 times per week	.1 kwh	X ___	= ___
___	**broiler (portable)** 1140 watts	twice a week	7 kwh	X ___	= ___
___	**can opener** 100 watts	3 uses per day	.03 kwh	X ___	= ___
___	**carving knife** 95 watts	twice a week	1 kwh	X ___	= ___
___	**clock** 2.5 watts	every day	2 kwh	X ___	= ___
___	**clothes dryer** 4900 watts	6 loads per week	83 kwh	X ___	= ___
___	**clothes washer (automatic)** 512 watts	6 loads per week	9 kwh	X ___	= ___
___	**coffee maker** 600 watts	once a day	5 kwh	X ___	= ___
___	**corn popper** 575 watts	2 uses per week	1 kwh	X ___	= ___
___	**curling iron** 40 watts	once a day	.3 kwh	X ___	= ___
___	**deep fat fryer*** 1200 watts	3 times a month	2 kwh	X ___	= ___
___	**dehumidifier** 257 watts	every day	31 kwh	X ___	= ___
___	**dishwasher** 1200 watts	25 loads per month	30 kwh	X ___	= ___
___	**disposer** 445 watts	every day	3 kwh	X ___	= ___
___	**electronic cleaner** 50 watts	every day	18 kwh	X ___	= ___
	electric heating**				
___	**egg cooker** 550 watts	5 times per week	1 kwh	X ___	= ___
	fans				
___	window 200 watts	2 hours every day	14 kwh	X ___	= ___
___	furnace or central air 270 watts	7 hours every day	59 kwh	X ___	= ___
___	**floor polisher** 305 watts	4 hours per month	1 kwh	X ___	= ___
___	**fondue/chafing dish*** 800 watts	once a month	.4 kwh	X ___	= ___
	freezer (15 cu. ft.)				
___	manual defrost 341 watts	every day	100 kwh	X ___	= ___
___	frost-free 440 watts	every day	147 kwh	X ___	= ___
___	**fry pan*** 1200 watts	15 uses	9 kwh	X ___	= ___
___	**garage door opener** (1/3 hp)	4 times per day	.3 kwh	X ___	= ___
___	**griddle*** 1200 watts	twice a week	4 kwh	X ___	= ___
	hair dryers				
___	soft bonnet 400 watts	twice a week	2 kwh	X ___	= ___
___	hard bonnet 900 watts	twice a week	4 kwh	X ___	= ___
___	hand held 600 watts	5 times per week	2 kwh	X ___	= ___
___	**hair setter/curler** 350 watts	3 times per week	1 kwh	X ___	= ___
___	**heating pad*** 60 watts	5 times per month	.3 kwh	X ___	= ___
___	**humidifier** 177 watts	every day	14 kwh	X ___	= ___
___	**ice cream freezer** 130 watts	once per month	.1 kwh	X ___	= ___
___	**ice crusher** 100 watts	twice a week	.04 kwh	X ___	= ___
___	**iron*** 1100 watts	2 hours per week	5 kwh	X ___	= ___
___	**juicer** 90 watts	once a day	.05 kwh	X ___	= ___
___	**knife sharpener** 40 watts	once a week	.01 kwh	X ___	= ___
___	**lighting**		108 kwh	X ___	= ___
___	**make-up mirror** 20 watts	once a day	.1 kwh	X ___	= ___
___	**microwave oven** 1450 watts	20 minutes per day	16 kwh	X ___	= ___
	mixer				
___	hand 80 watts	3 times	.1 kwh	X ___	= ___
___	stand 150 watts	twice a week	.2 kwh	X ___	= ___
___	**radio** 25 watts	2 hours every day	2 kwh	X ___	= ___
___	**range** 12,200 watts	for a family of 3	100 kwh	X ___	= ___
___	self-cleaning process*	twice a month	9 kwh	X ___	= ___
___	**roaster*** 1425 watts	once a month	5 kwh	X ___	= ___
	refrigerator (12 cu. ft.)				
___	manual defrost 241 watts	every day	61 kwh	X ___	= ___
___	frost-free 321 watts	every day	101 kwh	X ___	= ___
	refrigerator/freezer (14 cu. ft.)				
___	manual defrost 326 watts	every day	95 kwh	X ___	= ___
___	frost-free 615 watts	every day	152 kwh	X ___	= ___
___	**sewing machine** 75 watts	4 hours per week	1 kwh	X ___	= ___
___	**shaver** 15 watts	once a day	05 kwh	X ___	= ___
___	**shaving cream dispenser** 60 watts	every day	.03 kwh	X ___	= ___
___	**slow cooker** 200 watts	twice a month	3 kwh	X ___	= ___
___	**stereo/hi-fi** 109 watts	2 hours per day	9 kwh	X ___	= ___
___	**sun lamp** 290 watts	10 minutes every day	1 kwh	X ___	= ___
	television				
___	black & white, tube-type 160 watts	6 hours every day	29 kwh	X ___	= ___
___	black & white, solid state 55 watts	6 hours every day	10 kwh	X ___	= ___
___	color, tube-type 300 watts	6 hours every day	55 kwh	X ___	= ___
___	color, solid state 200 watts	6 hours every day	37 kwh	X ___	= ___
___	**toaster** 1400 watts	twice a day	4 kwh	X ___	= ___
___	**toothbrush** 1.1 watts	every day	1 kwh	X ___	= ___
___	**trash compactor** 400 watts	½ hour every day	4 kwh	X ___	= ___
___	**vacuum cleaner** 650 watts	10 minutes every day	4 kwh	X ___	= ___
___	**waffle iron*** 1200 watts	once a week	2 kwh	X ___	= ___
___	**warming tray** 140 watts	twice per month	1 kwh	X ___	= ___
	water heater				
___	general use	350 gallons per person for a family of 4	350 kwh	X ___	= ___
___	for clothes washer	6 loads per week	108 kwh	X ___	= ___
___	**water pump** 1000 watts	½ hour every day	15 kwh	X ___	= ___
___	**workshop and hobby equipment**	___	___	X ___	= ___

* Thermostatically controlled. Cost based on appliance estimated "On" time.

** Electric heating and air conditioning costs vary with each home. Many items affect an accurate estimate: size of home, type of system, amount of insulation, number of doors, windows, etc. On the above chart, kwh usage estimated for air conditioning represents an average for central Indiana for each of four cooling months. Kwh usage in northern Indiana would be lower; usage in southern Indiana would be higher. For information on **your** electric heating or cooling costs, call the nearest Public Service office.

6. Appliances

The larger the appliance the more power it will use, and so the bigger your bill. The following chart shows how many kilowatt hours are used by the equipment in a home based on monthly consumption by a family of four. By multiplying the kilowatt hours of your electric rate, you can estimate how much you spend monthly on each item. Of course, this is a rough estimation. Depending upon the size of your family, your living habits, and the health and age of your family, your kilowatt hours and electric bill could vary drastically from this chart. For those who have gas ranges, ovens, dryers, hot water heaters, etc. use this table.

Appliance	Est. thousand cu. ft./yr. at 12.39 lb./sq. in.
Range	12.6
Water Heater	33.7
Clothes Dryer (constant pilot)	8.6
Average Home Heating under average conditions	145.0
Gas Grill (depending upon use)	1.8-3.1
Air Conditioner	30.0

PLANNING AND DESIGN

Basically most of our appliances are found in kitchens, so some consideration should be given to its design. The major point in kitchen planning is to get maximum efficiency from all equipment and make use of outside elements which can help (or hinder) efficiency. (For additional details, see *Book of Successful Kitchens* by Patrick Galvin.) The plan shown indicates that wherever possible three separate areas should be established for (1) food storage; (2) preparation and cleanup; (3) cooking.

Storage

Install the refrigerator-freezer and separate freezer away from windows, radiators and heat-producing appliances. Locate refrigerator appliances in a level dry, cool and well-ventilated area. Make sure there is enough space behind and above the units to allow enough air circulation to the condenser.

Preparation and Cleanup

Locate the dishwasher as close to the water source as possible. You may even consider installing a separate water heater in the kitchen near the sink and dishwasher. It saves even more money if you insulate water pipes that pass through uninsulated areas. You pay less if your water is *kept* hot than to keep heating it up again.

Cooking

Locate the cooking range in an area away from refrigeration equipment. There's no need to pay money to heat your refrigeration units so that the cooling equipment in them has to work longer and harder. By

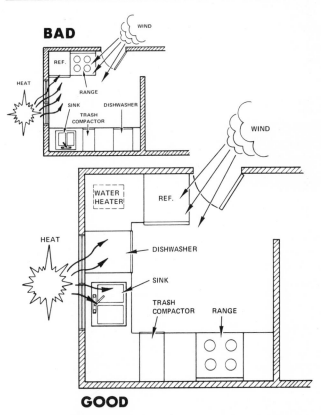

Three separate areas should be established in kitchens for maximum energy efficiency and dollar saving (courtesy of Whirlpool Corp.).

Compare your own estimated kwh use for each appliance with the average given, and adjust up or down. Multiply your average kwh use by your average cost per kwh. This will give you the estimated monthly cost to run each appliance (Courtesy of Public Service, Indiana).

installing a vent fan over the stove (see Chapter 4 on Ventilation) excess heat is drawn directly to the outside. You should, however, check all kitchen air leaks, such as around vents, which could cause heat loss in the winter and heat gains in the summer.

You'll notice that a good kitchen plan makes maximum use of the outside elements. The sun is utilized by placing a sink right near a window. Not only will natural sunlight save on light bills, but windows offer good ventilation for steam buildup when dishwashing. Why turn on a fan and pay for electricity if it isn't necessary? The refrigerator-freezer is placed where winds rather than heat can get at it. The winds provide good air circulation and will cut the electric bill by helping it run efficiently. But for the opposite reason, kitchen ranges and stoves are situated so that no drafts or cold appliances resist peak efficiency and drain your pocketbook.

But good kitchen management involves more than efficient design and layout. It means making the best use of these appliances. In turn this implies wise purchasing and maintenance as well. One of the first steps you should take is in the direction of off-peak hour use of as many of your appliances as possible. Of course you must know your local peak hours. They do vary in different parts of the U.S. In Vermont, for example, peak hours usually refers to winter use during the hours from 8 to 11 a.m. and again from 5 to 9 p.m. In Florida peak rates occur in summer when air conditioning use is at its highest, usually from 2 to 5 in the afternoon. In general, however, if you can avoid using appliances and other energy users during peak hours, you will lower your bills. Also:

- The hot water heater uses more energy than any other household appliance. Plan your water use during off-peak hours with a bit of scheduling for laundry, dishwashing, bathing (showers use less water than baths).
- Try to cook as much as possible during off-peak hours and simply warm food up before serving meals.
- Ironing, hair-drying, vacuuming, etc. can usually be fitted into an off-peak hour schedule with a little effort.

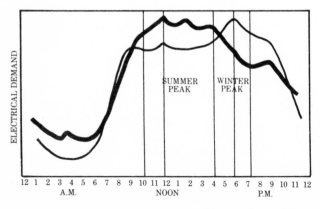

Boston Edison

Making the most of your appliances and cutting your energy bill is often no effort at all. During the winter in cold climates you may prefer to turn on your dishwasher in the evening (after peak hours). The humidity from your dishwasher will be diffused through the house making lower temperatures more acceptable. During the summer when humidity is the enemy, turn on the dishwasher very early in the morning, before heat buildup, or just before you're ready to go to bed.

During the winter when your kitchen is at its busiest, you can probably lower the thermostat without anyone feeling it. This would occur from about 3 p.m. to 8 p.m., a time when children are arriving home from school and taking milk and cookies and when dinner is prepared and eaten. The refrigerator is generating more (it's being used more) and it is dispersing heat (feel the bottom where the heat is pushed out from the motor) as well as humidity from the circulating coils. The stove or oven is probably in operation, too.

LOWERING YOUR ELECTRIC RATE

The skyrocketing cost of power is one result of the recognized energy crisis. In order to keep prices under control and to make our current supply of energy last until new supplies are available, we must learn to manage our current rate of energy consumption differently. The studies made underscore the problem; they show that 37 percent of total energy consumption is spent on residential and private auto owners. With those figures it's foolish to think that private consumers don't control a big hunk of the market.

Unfortunately electricity cannot be stored in large quantities. It must be generated from chemical, hydro or nuclear energy as it is needed. Your electric utility must maintain, therefore, enough electrical-generation equipment to meet the peak load of the year, even though much of this equipment is not required during the remainder of the year. And this is how your rates are figured–at the peak hour of the peak season of the year. (Most companies have different summer and winter rates.) Naturally, this rate is extremely high, but the electrical equipment which stands idle much of the time must be there for peak periods and so we must pay for it all year 'round.

Scheduling the use of electrical appliances when community power demands are low will contribute to lower rates in the future, or at least stop substantial increases, as well as improve electrical efficiency. During off-peak hours, economical high-efficiency equipment is available to make electricity, thus bypassing the need to use expensive low-efficiency equipment kept by companies solely for the purpose of auxiliary power when absolutely needed. As more and more people use off-peak hours, obviously that "peak" lowers (see illustration) hopefully along with your electric rate. Some power companies are pushing off-peak-hours use by putting special meters on homes offering lower off-peak hour rates and higher rates when the homeowner uses power during prime time. Find out your local peak hours; each area has its own.

In hot weather the opposite will hold true. No cooking should be attempted unless it's fast broiling or sauteing. (Try backyard barbecuing—even if you want to eat in your air conditioned dining room.) Long-oven cooking is not advisable unless done early in the morning. All your cold food preparation such as salads, iced tea, etc., should be done in the morning as well.

BUYING POWER

The best advice is BUYER BEWARE. Before purchasing any appliance, large or small, check on the following.

1. Know your family's lifestyle. Don't be influenced by "extra" features if your family has no need of them. Do, however, understand how much time and effort your family is willing to devote to appliance maintenance. You may want to spend money for those proven advantages.

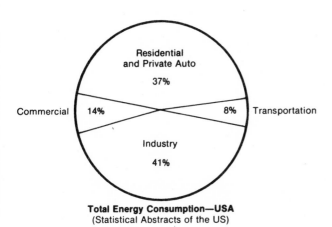

Total Energy Consumption—USA
(Statistical Abstracts of the US)

The following chart shows how the 37 percent consumed by individual users is further divided to meet the needs of the average household.

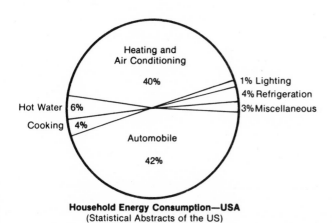

Household Energy Consumption—USA
(Statistical Abstracts of the US)

2. Study all appliance information in magazines, and if possible manufacturer spec sheets. Then shop various brands and different models in various stores. Ask salespersons for help if you're confused. Ask questions, especially about the EER rating (see Chapter 3).

3. Look for the seal of approval of the regulating body such as American Gas Association Blue Star Certification.

4. Compare warranties. Does one appliance have a warranty which assures "parts are serviced" while another reads "nonmoving parts are replaced." Find out what each warranty means in terms of money and responsibility.

5. Only buy from reputable dealers who can back up their appliances. You may now wish to ask about financial arrangements.

6. Make careful arrangements if your appliance must be installed by a serviceperson. Make sure you receive proper instructions on how to run the machine and that it is in good running order when the installer leaves.

7. If you have purchased the machine and you do run into trouble, call the dealer. If he cannot help, write the manufacturer. If that doesn't work, contact: Major Appliance Consumer Action Panel, 20 North Wacker Drive, Chicago, Illinois 60606; phone 312-236-3165.

STOVES & OVENS

Cutting your energy bills means taking a hard look at the major appliances you have or are going to buy in the future. In the cooking department there is a vast selection facing the uninformed. Will you have a gas or electric range and oven? Are you going to use microwave cookery? Do you want a self-cleaning or a continuous-cleaning oven?

For starters, the styles of ovens and ranges are shown here. Generally, a natural gas oven (if available in your locality) is cheaper to operate. Some people find that their electric rates make it less expensive to operate a gas oven/range on bottled gas. Be sure to find out rate comparisons from your utility company. You can figure you use your oven and range about 239 hours per year. For efficiency, however, electricity is better; there are no wasted energy units, as there are with gas oven pilot lights.

But aside from some personal advantages for special features such as wall ovens, smooth surface ranges, rotisseries, griddles or warming shelves (be sure you want them and see if they are tricky to repair), there are definite pro's and con's on some main features. Both gas and electric cooking appliances offer these features which can cut your energy bill:

    (1) automatic oven-cleaning.;
    (2) thermostatically controlled burners;
    (3) pilotless gas stoves; and
    (4) microwave ovens.

FREE STANDING   SLIDE-IN

DROP-IN   EYE-LEVEL OR HIGH OVEN

BUILT-IN

Five styles of stoves from which to choose (courtesy Pacific Gas and Electric Co. Home Economics Dept.).

Automatic cleaning. There are two basic systems of automatic oven cleaning—self-cleaning and continuous clean. The continuous clean process is called the catalytic method; it uses chemical coating on the walls or panels and contains a catalyst of substances which oxidizes stains at normal baking temperatures. Although the advantage of this system is that no extra power of your energy dollar is spent cleaning the oven, often spots do not disappear at normal oven temperatures. They will usually disappear at temperatures of about 450 degrees. Sometimes the oven must be turned up to this temperature for several hours to rid the oven of soil completely. This will raise your energy bill. But the biggest disadvantage is that on many of the continuous clean ovens there is no warranty on the life of the catalytic cleaning action. Also, because the walls and panels of the continuous clean oven are treated chemically, you must be extremely careful as to the type of cleaning agents you use if you decide to clean your oven manually.

The self-cleaning oven uses a pyrolytic method of cleaning. The soil is decomposed with controlled high heat. The cleaning cycle takes from 1½ to 3 hours at temperatures from 850 to 1,000 degrees. You lock the door and turn the controls to "clean" (most doors cannot be unlocked during the process), and at the end of the cycle you open the oven and wipe up the residue ash with a paper towel. The disadvantages of this type of oven are that it costs more to purchase and it costs money every time you run the self-cleaning operation. But many experts say these disadvantages are offset because of the extra insulation put into these ovens (the extra insulation makes the stove more expensive to build and the cost is passed on to the consumer). The advantage of extra insulation means that there is much less heat loss during normal baking, which can cut many kilowatt hours of money off your bill. You can also choose when you wish to clean your oven. If you never wish to turn on the clean cycle, you can clean the oven manually using any of the recommended oven cleaners—the porcelain walls and panels are not treated chemically. Warranties on this type of automatic oven cleaning are available.

Thermostatically controlled. Another feature which can cut your energy bill is a thermostatically controlled burner. You set a temperature (as you do your oven) and the heating unit controls the temperature at the same level—going higher or lower in order to maintain it. You can cut about 11 percent off your fuel bill using this handy little gadget.

Pilotless gas stoves. These operate on a spark ignition system. With this system, you eliminate the pilot lights and you can expect to cut your stove bill by 30 percent. This feature cannot be added to a gas stove or range already in a home. The original purchase will cost more than a stove using a pilot light system (about $75 more).

Microwave cookery. Not intended to replace conventional cooking methods; some types of food do not adapt well to the speed. But whenever you can use a microwave oven you can be sure that you'll be cutting your bill in a big way. By cooking your food electronically, you'll cut the amount of time by $2/3$ and you'll use about half the energy as a regular oven.

Because this oven is meant to act as a complementary cooking appliance there is no cause to complain about the lack of a "browned" look as foods come out of the oven. Brown them conventionally. Some companies are now producing an oven that does both conventional and microwave cooking in one oven.

The principle behind the savings on microwave ovens is that only the food absorbs the microwaves and becomes hot. But it is time, and not temperature, that will vary in microwave cookery. There is no temperature control. The time is related to the food's starting temperature, volume and density. Because only the food is affected by the microwaves (they are like fast radio waves), the air, the surfaces of the oven compartment and the utensils remain at room temperature. This is a great advantage for summer cooking, especially if you run an air conditioner.

Besides the new microwave-conventional range combination, there are many portable countertop styles or those which can be built in. They require no special outlets other than a standard 115 volt three-prong outlet, which is always grounded.

For those who want to conserve the maximum amount of utility energy (the other extreme from microwave ovens), the old-fashioned wood burning stove may be the answer. The stove not only serves as a cooking appliance but actually heats rooms comfortably whenever it's burning wood. The installation and chimney problems should be carefully though out, along with the inconveniences of wood chopping and storage, fire-starting, smoking, and cleaning.

Riding the Range

By using a few of the following tips you can trim down your energy costs.

- Never use your stove (conventional type) for room-heating purposes.
- Don't open oven doors while baking. There's a 20 percent heat loss.
- Don't use aluminum foil to line oven unless manufacturer instructions permit it. This can reduce circulation and cut down the oven's efficiency. For the same reason, arrange pans so that they do not touch each other or the oven walls; make sure pans are not directly above one another.
- Whenever possible, turn on a self-cleaning oven right after cooking in it, while it's still hot. Less

Pilotless gas stoves can cut 30 percent off your bill (courtesy Caloric Corp.).

By cooking your food in a microwave oven, you can cut your cooking time by two-thirds and use only half the amount of energy as a conventional oven. Electronic cooking is not intended, however, to completely replace your regular oven (courtesy of Frigidaire).

energy dollars will be used to get it to the heat-cleaning stage.

- Use thawed or partially thawed foods. They cook faster.
- Don't preheat oven. Most dishes do not require it. Those that do only need 10 minutes of preheat.
- Try to cook as many things at one time in your oven as possible. Oven dishes with temperatures of plus or minus 25 degrees can be cooked together.
- Choose pans that fit the range unit—flat bottoms, straight sides with tight lids. Dull dirty pans won't attract electric heat as quickly as shiny clean ones.
- Don't turn on range before the pan is on the burner.
- Use minimum amount of water, especially when cooking frozen vegetables; bring to a boil quickly in a covered pan with high heat; switch to lowest setting needed.
- Water boils faster in a covered pot—20 percent savings.
- Try lower heat for oven roast, 325 degrees. This can reduce meat shrinkage and spattering grease, along with your bill.
- Use top-of-the-range cooking for faster jobs. An electric range uses 1.5 kilowatts while the oven uses 5 or more. But for long-cooking recipes, your oven is cheaper because less heat is lost in the confined area.
- If your range has two ovens, use the smaller whenever possible. It uses less power.
- Use leftover heat from oven to warm plates or rolls.
- Increase your electric range efficiency by keeping clean reflector pans under the surface units.
- Never preheat the broiler; it's a total waste. Try broiling as many things as possible at the same time. Look at broiler "meals."
- Use pressure cooker (if you have one) whenever possible. It cuts down cooking time and energy dollars.
- Cast iron, copper and stainless steel require lower heat setting than does aluminum.
- On electric surface burners, you can often turn units off 5 minutes ahead of finished cooking time and let the food continue to cook as the heat gradually diminishes.
- Whenever possible use your microwave oven if you have one.
- Bake in glass or ceramic pans whenever possible. You can then reduce your oven setting 25 degrees.
- If your gas range produces a yellow flame, it's not working at peak efficiency. Call your repairman (flame should be blue).

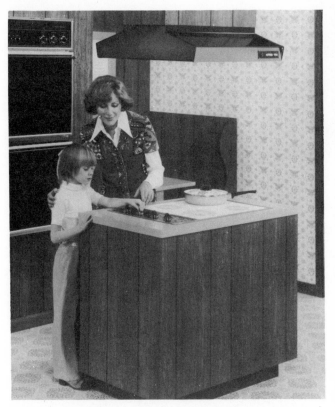

A new concept in surface cooking is glass-ceramic—a smooth, flat white finish containing from two to four heating units with sunburst designs. A thermostatic sensor concealed beneath each unit maintains heat setting. When turned off, it wipes clean easily and provides extra counter space (courtesy of Whirlpool Corp.).

Two major points which are obvious should be mentioned here. First, make sure your stove is turned off whenever it's not in use. Second, keep it as clean and as in good repair as possible. Make sure you read all the manufacturer's do's and don'ts. If your stove isn't working properly, call a serviceperson and have it checked.

REFRIGERATORS & FREEZERS

Buying a refrigerator or freezer, or combination of the two, may mean making some hard choices between saving energy dollars and cutting down on conveniences. Of course this often depends on the size and lifestyle of your family. But keep in mind that your energy bills are affected by the size (cubic feet) of the refrigerator-freezer, the freezer temperature, the defrost, the shape and placement of the freezer and the extra optional features.

The bigger the unit, the more energy it uses and the higher your electric bill. Eight cubic feet of refrigerator space is usually considered adequate for a family of two; add one cubic foot for each additional person plus two more feet for a family that entertains frequently. If there is a freezer compartment, estimate about 2 cubic feet per person. For separate freezers, space is figured at 6 cubic feet per person. A freezer set to run at 15 degrees will cost less to operate than one which operates at 0 degrees. A self-defrosting refrigerator-freezer will cost more to run —using up to 50 percent more energy than a manual defrost model. And the larger the freezer compartment in the refrigerator unit, the more expensive the operating cost. A side-by-side style refrigerator-freezer costs you more operating money than a conventional two-door upright. A freezer chest offers a lower monthly electric bill than an upright model of the same cubic capacity. But only you can decide if an ice-cube dispenser on the outside of your refrigerator is worth the extra operating expense. A frill may turn into a money-saver; for example, if your children like cold drinks and are constantly opening the refrigerator to get them. The foam insulation is usually of higher quality and may take dollars off your electric bill in the long run. Investigate all the possibilities of types and styles until you find one that fits your family's needs.

Many companies are trying to overcome the problem of higher energy costs coupled with convenience features. If you prefer a self-defrosting or no-frost refrigerator-freezer unit, there is a special energy-reducing switch which turns down small heaters that reduce humidity inside the appliance. This switch is only used when humidity is low; some switches are turned on manually while others come on automatically. It is said to save the owner at least $35 per year in comparison to the regular frost-free units.

The Cold Facts

Using your refrigerator and freezer to maximize efficiency and cut your energy bills isn't difficult. It takes a bit of maintenance and common sense.

- Avoid unnecessarily "cold" settings in your unit. Milk should taste pleasantly cold to your family and ice cream in the freezer should be firm.
- Check door seals for tightness so that no warm air is leaking in or cold air going out. Place a dollar bill between the seal and cabinet. It should not slide out easily. Check at various points on your door. If the seal isn't good, call your repairman.
- Plan ahead and take out as many items from the refrigerator or freezer at one time as possible.
- Defrost non-frostfree models regularly; *before* the ice buildup exceeds ¼ of an inch. Frost acts as an insulator, making the refrigerator consume more power to maintain temperatures.
- Clean the condenser fins (coils) at least twice a year. Dust reduces their efficiency. Be sure to unplug the unit. (The condenser coils are located behind the bottom grille panel or in the back of the unit.)
- Keep your freezer section and your separate freezer unit as full as you can. Less cold air is lost during door openings because the frozen food helps retain the cold. If your freezer isn't filled to capacity, fill some empty milk cartons with water and put them in your freezer.
- Use your refrigerator to full capacity but allow enough space between items for free air circulation; don't block air vents.
- If your model has a power-saver or power-economizer switch, use it whenever possible according to manufacturer's instructions.
- During vacations leave your refrigerator fairly empty and set a slightly warmer temperature or if feasible, empty entirely and cut off power with refrigerator open.
- Always cover liquids stored in frostfree refrigerators. Uncovered liquids draw more moisture

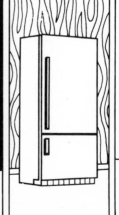

CONVENTIONAL   PORTABLE   TOP FREEZER   BOTTOM FREEZER   SIDE FREEZER

Different styles of refrigerator-freezer units can affect your electric bill. A side by side style refrigerator-freezer, for example, costs you more to run than a conventional two-door upright (courtesy of Pacific Gas and Electric Home Economics Dept.).

into the air making the unit work longer and so increase your bill.

- Let hot dishes cool to near room temperature before they are placed in the refrigerator or freezer.
- If you keep your old refrigerator as backup storage, plug it in only when actually in use. (Make sure it's safe for children.)
- If you have a no-frost or self-defrosting refrigerator, it will usually have a condensation drain. It should be examined regularly and kept clean and free from obstructions. If this drain becomes clogged for prolonged periods of time, ice will build up on the coils and impair the unit's operation.
- Don't freeze too much food at once. Put no more unfrozen food into your freezer than will freeze within 24 hours; this is usually about 2 or 3 pounds of food to each cubic foot. Overloading forces it to run overtime and may overheat the motor. Foods frozen too slowly may spoil. You may, however, turn controls to a colder setting and then as food freezes turn it back to normal.
- Remove paper wrappings from foods before putting them in the refrigerator. Paper acts as insulation.
- Plug the refrigerator-freezer into an outlet that is not being used for any other appliance. Do not use an extension cord.
- In the event a freezer unit is "off" for a period of time, a well-filled freezer should keep foods frozen 24 to 48 hours, depending on room temperatures. But keep the freezer door closed!

UPRIGHT FREEZER

CHEST FREEZER

An upright freezer takes up less floor space than a chest freezer but the upright uses more energy to operate (Pacific Gas and Electric Co. Home Economics Dept.).

New energy-efficient refrigerator freezers are now available in frost-free models from most manufacturers. Better insulation plus a power-saving control device save you about $35 per year compared to old-style free units (courtesy Sears, Robeuck and Co.).

WASHERS AND DRYERS

Again, choosing a washer and dryer will depend on your family's needs and the space you have for laundry equipment—front loader or top loader, portable or combination machine. There are, however, features which could help cut your energy bill. You might want to find out if the washing machine you're thinking of buying has a water temperature control, a water level control and a water suds saver. More personal preferences involve such features as a gentle cycle or automatic dispensers.

Your future dryer will usually have all the features necessary for economic operation. The main difference will be found in automatic or manual selection. In other words, you can manually set the timer to work for 50 minutes and manually decide that it's a permanent press load and push the proper heat setting for it. Or, there are dryers which automatically set both the drying time and temperature control dial (you, of course, have to work that). This dial is a combined thermostat and timer. If you are purchasing a gas dryer you can save operating costs by buying one which has a spark-ignition system.

The washing machine can cost more money to run that you estimate. In terms of electric kilowatts, it appears that you're paying much more to run your dryer (see chart on first page of this Chapter) but your washing machine costs are hidden. Look at how much it costs to run your water heater (quick recovery units are even higher) and your water pump. These costs must be counted in the washing process. When you select a washer it's wise to look closely at the water level control. One level for large washes, another for medium loads, another for regular and another for small. A feature that will save you using unnecessary water is an important bill-cutter. Large families may want to investigate water suds saver feature. This permits the use of warm water for more than one load—especially useful where a number of loads are washed in sequence. Another bill cutter is water temperature control. Look at your hot-water heater costs and figure out that a washer which can be set to warm or cold water temperature has an invaluable money-saving feature built into it.

Laundry Lighteners

The placement of your laundry equipment will affect your bill. By placing your washing machine near the source of hot water, you'll be saving energy dollars. And if your dryer is installed in a heated area of your home it may cost you less money to run it. In an unheated garage or uninsulated utility room, the heating elements of the dryer will remain on longer during cold weather. If you do place the dryer in a heated part of your home, make sure it's properly vented to the outside. Venting prevents buildup of

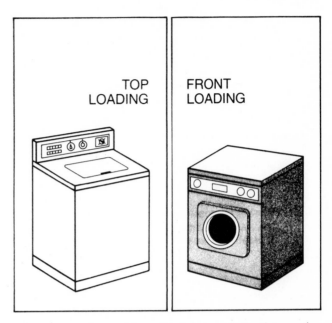

Selecting a washer and dryer depends on your family's needs and space for equipment. How and where they are installed influences operating costs (courtesy of Pacific Gas and Electric Co. Home Economics Dept.).

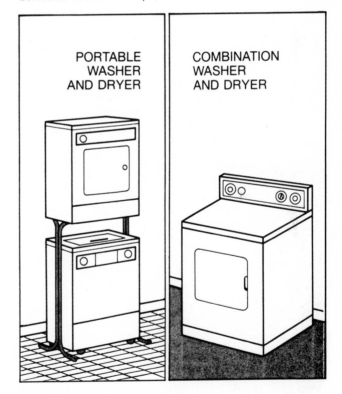

excess moisture in the laundry area that can cause mildew and warping. Venting reduces drying time and also removes heat, lessening your air conditioning requirements during hot weather. For best results keep vent tubing as short as possible. The following tips are for everyday use of laundry equipment.

- Sort clothes according to fabric and color; you'll save money on hot water and electricity by washing and drying similar items together (delicate clothes need shorter cycles than work clothes).
- If you have water-level control, choose the correct water-level setting for the size of the wash load. Don't use more water than you need.
- If you have no water level selector, wait until you have a full load of clothes before washing. Each full cycle can cost as much as 5 kilowatt hours.
- Whenever possible use cold or warm water in your wash cycle.
- Beware of overloading your washer and dryer. The washer will undergo extra strain and will not operate efficiently. The clothes will wrinkle excessively in the dryer.
- Don't dry clothes longer than necessary. Overdrying clothes not only means higher electric or gas bills, but it means wrinkled, yellowed clothes which wear out quickly.
- Dry your clothes in consecutive loads while the dryer is still warm.
- Measure detergents for your washer carefully. Oversudsing makes your washer work harder and longer.
- If you have a laundry tub next to your washer, save the hot sudsy water from the wash to clean garden tools, mops, barbecue racks, etc.
- After wash is completed, turn off the water faucets. This avoids undue pressure on the hoses.
- Clean the lint filter on your washer and dryer after each load. This makes equipment run at peak efficiency, and reduces drying time, too.
- Don't dry clothes thoroughly that you want damp for ironing.
- Make sure your dryer has its own electric circuit.
- The washer should be on a separate, grounded circuit.

DISHWASHERS

From built-ins to portables, dishwashers are tops on the list of kitchen cleanup aids. It takes more hot water to wash dishes by hand than it does to run the same amount of dishes through the dishwasher. The key word in dishwashers is efficiency. Like laundry equipment, models which can help save on the amount of water (and it's usually expensive hot water) are preferable. Some dishwashers now use warm and cold water during certain cycles. Look carefully at the one you intend to purchase; the amount of water—warm, hot, or cold—can vary from 10 gallons to 18.5 gallons in different dishwashers. Those which can be stopped for the drying cycle so that you can let the dishes drain dry with the excess heat from washing will, of course, save money on electrical drying costs. Some dishwashers now turn off automatically during the drying process for a certain amount of time. And there is no need to set your hot water heater higher than 150 degrees. The extra heat costs you money and is unnecessary to clean your dishes. Again, as with your clothes washer, the nearer your dishwasher is to the source of hot water, the cheaper your bills will be. For everyday use, the following tips can save you money.

- Operate the dishwasher only when you have a full load.
- Normally, soiled dishes do not require rinsing. But if dishes are left until dishwasher is full, watch out for excessive amounts of starchy and hard bits of food on plates and flatwear. Rinse those off.
- Do not set water heater above 150 degrees.
- For greatest efficiency place dishes so soiled area faces source of washing action. Avoid nesting items.
- Measure detergent (one specifically made for dishwashers) carefully. Too much or too little will reduce efficiency.

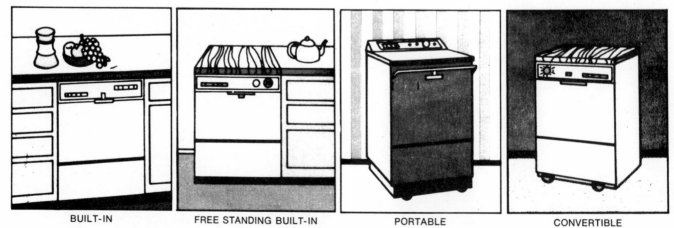

BUILT-IN   FREE STANDING BUILT-IN   PORTABLE   CONVERTIBLE

No matter what style of dishwasher you choose energy-saving devices should be included (courtesy of Pacific Gas and Electric Co. Home Economics Dept.).

- Check the filter screen over the drain of the dishwasher. Remove any particles. Debris in the dishwasher pump can hamper the machine's efficiency.
- Avoid using the dishwasher as a plate warmer; it's more economical to use the oven's stored heat for this purpose.
- Whenever possible cut off dishwasher drying cycle and dry by air. You will, however, lose the sterilized effect.

Read your manufacturer's instructions and follow care and maintenance closely. Refer to it if any problems arise, before calling a repairman.

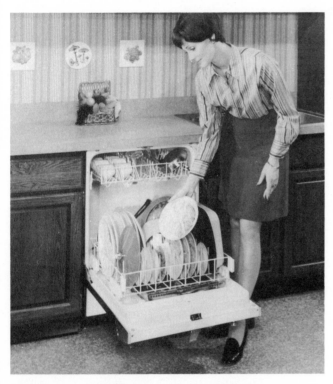

Manufacturers are taking another look at high-energy appliances—especially those which have great kitchen appeal such as a dishwasher. They are reducing operating costs with lower water temperatures and shorter washing and drying cycles (courtesy of Whirlpool Corp.).

PORTABLE APPLIANCES

As energy costs rise and seem to be going out of sight, many people are wondering if small portable appliances are simply an added burden to the electric bill. Not necessarily. Many portable appliances do specialized jobs with little mess and less electricity than major appliances (cooking a meal in your electric skillet instead of your range is much cheaper). In some cases small

appliances may actually save quite a bit more energy than when done "manually." An electric shaver takes less electricity than would be needed to heat water for a lather shave.

Items such as electric clocks are low wattage users and they don't contribute very much to your bill. Items that are used for brief periods such as carving knives, tooth brushes and small tools have very little effect on your bill. For example, a color television set uses more electricity in one hour than a can opener would use all year. A frost-free refrigerator uses more electric energy in one day than a carving knife uses in six years. An electric shaver can be used for three years on less energy than it takes to run a food freezer for three hours.

Using many small appliances can add to your bill, while using others properly can defray the cost of a large appliance. Some people find it worthwhile to choose appliances which serve more than one function (electric skillets can be used for frying, pan broiling, sauteeing, stewing, baking, roasting and sometimes broiling). Some appliances also double as serving dishes, reducing the number of dishes in your dishwasher. Toaster ovens can serve a dual role in toasting and baking or defrosting for less money than it would cost to use your range.

"RATING" YOUR ELECTRIC EQUIPMENT

Obviously, on all your electrical purchases you will want to get as high an Energy Efficiency Ratio (EER) as you can. Usually the EER rating is attached to the new appliances as well as being stamped on the metal plate of air conditioners. The higher the operating efficiency the higher the number attached to EER, and the less expensive it will be for you to operate. If the wattage of the unit is not listed on the item, you can find it quickly by multiplying the listed amperes by the voltage the unit operates on, either 120 or 240 volts. Thus 10 amperes times 120 volts equals 1,200 watts. An EER of 10 is great; 8 to 9 is good; 6 to 7 is passable. An appliance with an EER rating of 8.8, as compared to one that rates 6.3, would cost you about 28 percent less on your bill.

But before buying any portable appliance you should make sure that it will meet a real need in your family and will be able to do the job more efficiently than it's being done now. New appliances have an energy efficiency ratio which rate their energy use. Your new appliance should also have an Underwriters Laboratory registered symbol indicating the appliance meets their safety standards. Most important of all, is your house adequately wired to accommodate these electrical appliances?

A 100-ampere service is the recommended minimum capacity which supplies a basic electric capacity of 24,000 watts (240 volt supply). This would supply electricity for lighting, portable appliances plus most major equipment. You should, however, know the wattage of the appliance you use; never connect more than 1,650 watts on any electrical circuit at one time. Below is a list of the average range of wattage for some portable appliances.

Heated Serving Tray		Broiler/	
or Table	100-200	Rotisserie . . .1320-1650	
Ice Cream		Casserole	1350
Freezer	115-200	Coffee	
Mixer,		Maker 475-1500	
Portable	100-150	Cooker/	
Mixer,		Fryer 1350-1500	
Standard . . .	100-200	Corn Popper . .	650
Roaster-		Fondue Pot . . .	500-800
Oven	870-1650	Frypan 1000-1500	
Table Range . .1000-1650		Griddle 1300-1500	
Toaster	750-1650	Hairsetter	600-650
Waffle Baker . .	660-1400	Hair Dryer	400-1000
Blender	300-1200	Hand Iron	900-1200
Table Broiler . .1000-1650			

Consider the wattage of the appliance you are thinking of buying. Select the one with the lowest wattage that will still perform satisfactorily. A four-slice toaster takes 1500 to 1600 watts, a two-slice toaster only 750 watts.

Similarly to large appliances, different styles can increase or decrease your electric bill. For example a large black and white TV costs you more money to run than a smaller screen would. Solid-state units (black and white) cost one-third less money to operate than the filament tube units. And color solid-state TV uses about two-thirds of the energy of a color tube set. Any color TV will use more electricity than a black and white TV of a similar model. Instant turn-on features use more electricity constantly—whether the set is on or off. This feature usually costs more to purchase, too.

Also keep in mind that rechargeable appliances generally will cost you more to operate than those that run directly from the electrical outlet. Appliances which are thermostatically controlled are usually more efficient. Here are some economical ways to run portables.

- Abandon your range whenever possible. Use small appliances such as toaster, electric frypans, crockpots, etc., which use less power and so cost less to operate.

- Unplug your instant turn-on TV if you are away from home for a length of time. Many of these sets have a switch on the back so that you can turn the instant-on feature "off."
- Incessantly flicking the TV on and off causes unnecessary wear and tear and increases maintenance costs.
- Don't entertain an empty room. Be sure to turn off the TV, stereo or radio when no one is in the room or listening to it.
- Iron large amounts of clothes at one time. Every time you heat up an iron, you spend money.
- Reduce iron's warm-up time by first ironing fabrics that require the lowest temperature setting. Advance to medium and then the high-setting fabrics.
- Keep portable cooking appliances out of drafts for maximum efficiency.
- Vacuum cleaner bags should be emptied before they are overloaded. This keeps your machine operating at peak efficiency.
- Low wattage slow cookers let you cook a meal all day while you're away from home, but cost only a few cents worth of electricity.
- Automatic coffee makers allow you to brew coffee or heat water for instant beverages without heating an entire range surface unit, with one-half the energy cost.
- Use toaster ovens for baking small amounts of food. They use about one-half the wattage of a conventional oven.
- An electric blanket may allow you to set back your thermostat at night and save on heating costs.
- Make sure you turn off all appliances when you are finished using them (electric blankets, heating pads, etc).
- Don't use hot water when operating your disposer. Cold water solidifies grease which is then ground up and washed away.
- Portable electric heaters should be thermostatically controlled. Limit their use to temporary heating; they aren't designed for full-time heating operation.
- Keeping the coffee pot on all day puts a drain on energy dollars.

Maintenance and a bit of loving care will keep your appliances operating in good order. Accessibility and easy storage also contribute to lower bills. You will use small appliances instead of large ones only if the small ones are conveniently located.

Most people would agree that manufacturers' instruction manuals are not the most interesting reading matter you can find around your home. And the temptation to avoid reading them until you have trouble with your appliance is very great. Most of us manage to avoid it, but the trouble often could have been prevented by reading the manual when the appliance was delivered. These manuals not only give you a trouble-free run for your money, tthey also give you the lowdown on the way to get the most benefit out of your appliance. You may want to put all your manufacturers' manuals together in a folder near your guarantees and warranties.

WIRING

It's more than probable that 4 out of 5 homes are suffering from inadequate wiring. This is not surprising because the average family is using 4 times as much electricity today as it did 25 years ago—and within the next 10 years may double its electric use. Insufficient electric power in your home is costing you money. If you are operating at 90 percent capacity, it takes your toaster 1/5th longer to toast adequately and 1/5th longer for your electric fry-pan to heat. You get about 1/3rd less light from your incandescent bulbs and so on, down the line. There are certain symptoms which appear in homes with inadequate wiring. See if your house passes the wiring test.

- Do lights flicker and dim when appliances are turned on?
- Do appliances operate slowly or not as well as they should?
- Do heating appliances (toasters, irons) warm up too slowly?
- Do fuses blow or circuit breakers trip too frequently?
- Do radios or stereo receivers fade or sound scratchy when other appliances are turned on?
- Does TV picture shrink in size or "wince" when other appliances are turned on?
- Are there too few outlets and switches where you need them?

- Do you have multiple "octopus" connections to serve several appliances?
- Are extension cords strung around rooms in order to connect lamps or appliances?

If you have answered "yes" to several questions there is probably not enough electric power being fed into your home. Electricity travels through wires as water does through pipes. There is a large-sized main line which carries electricity to your area; smaller wires branch off and lead to houses such as yours, to your electric meter and service entrance (circuit panel box); these in turn branch off into different circuits to supply you with enough power for all your electric appliances including lighting.

But as with water pipes, each wire can carry just so much electricity. The limits are set by size—the larger the wire, the larger the amount of current (measured in amperes) it will carry. Thus, if a certain appliance is using most of the electricity a wire can deliver, plugging in another appliance on the same circuit will cause the fuse to blow or circuit breaker to trip, or load the circuit so heavily that neither will get enough current to operate at maximum efficiency. Larger wires delivering more current are used for major appliances such as dryers or electric ranges; smaller wires with less current supply smaller appliances and so on.

The final check on your home's wiring involves noting three basic points. (1) You should have a three-wire service entrance, at least 100 amperes—150 or 200 is even better, to carry all the power you'll need now and in the future. (2) You should have enough branches of general purpose circuits for each 375 to 500 square feet of floor space, enough small appliance circuits—3 for kitchen-laundry room, dining room, etc., and separate large appliance circuits for each major appliance on your circuit fuse box. (3) You should have enough switches and outlets—one for every 12 feet of wall space and in your kitchen one for every 4 feet (these should be three-prong grounded receptacles).

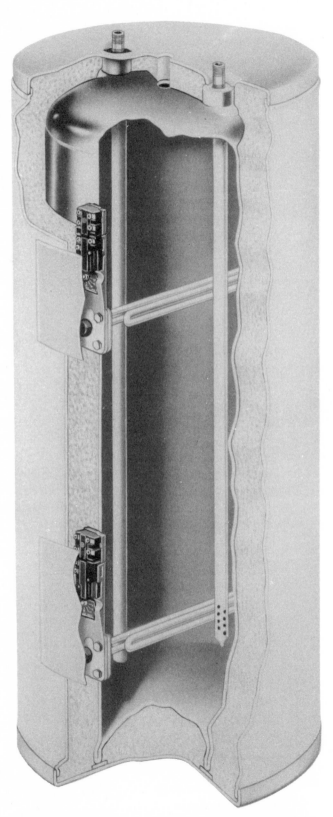

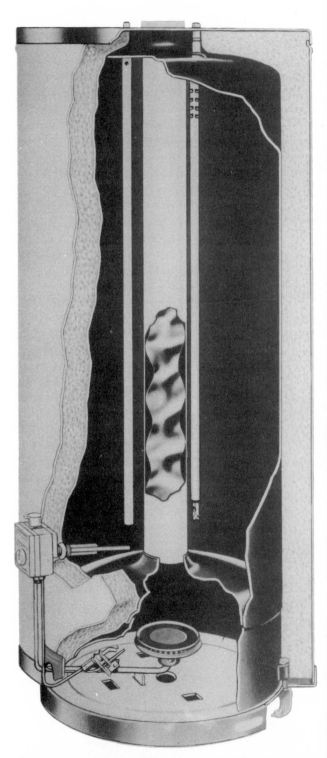

Cut away view of a typical gas-fired water heater (on right) and an electric hot water heater (at left). These units are relatively simple and you should get to know yours. Control unit in gas heater is at lower left and in electric heater it is found beneath plates on top and bottom of the tank. You should use these control units; you can turn your heater to lowest setting for general use (120°) or switch the entire unit off when you are away from home for several days (A. O. Smith Co.).

7. Hot Water

Because the hot water heater is usually tucked away in a corner of the cellar or in a closet, it is seldom seen or noticed. Yet year in and year out, operating on either gas, oil or electricity, it produces hot water and also chalks up a substantial part of the total energy bill. Estimates place the total at 13 percent to 15 percent. If your annual energy bill is $800, the hot water heater is probably costing you about $104 or more a year.

HOW TO SURVEY YOUR SYSTEM

Before you can begin saving money with your hot water system, it must be surveyed to find points of waste which can then be corrected. A survey of this system begins with the heater and includes pipes, plumbing fixtures, dishwasher and clothes washer, and of course how you and your family use the system. Ask yourself the following:

- Is hot water actually required for the task or area to which it is being supplied?
- What temperature of hot water is *really* needed in a specific location?
- Can the amount of hot water used be reduced?
- Are long piping runs needed to supply particular locations?
- Do pipes run through uninsulated areas? Are the pipes insulated?
- How is the water heated? Is there a cheaper way?
- Are the tank capacity and rating of burners, or heating element, properly sized to best meet the needs of your family?

Depending on how you answer the above questions, you can begin saving dollars right off. Often hot water goes to areas of the home where it is not really needed. A basement wash tub is typical. In an area such as this, cold running water is just as effective. You can turn the hot water faucet off.

Water temperature is probably the trickiest waste problem. There are three settings on standard hot water heaters: high, medium and low. If yours is set on high, you're wasting money. The high setting will give you a temperature range of 180 degrees or above; the middle range is 140 to 160 degrees and the lower setting is about 120 degrees. If you analyze the situation carefully, you will discover that you rarely use or need the highest temperature of 180. For showers, baths and washing dishes by hand (or any situation where you must immerse any part of your body in water), 120 degrees will be more than adequate; probably you would have to combine that heated 120 degree water with cold water to tolerate it comfortably. Heating water and then cooling it before you use it is a needless waste of energy dollars.

If you have electric appliances such as dishwashing machines or clothes washers, the previously required setting of 160 to 180 degrees has gone by the board (see chapter 6). Most manufacturers have come up with a successful compromise so that hot water heaters need never be set at more than 150 in order to achieve an efficient cleaning process. Some may even be set lower. If you wish to be even more economical and keep the setting at the lowest range of 120 degrees, all that's required is a little adjustment in your thinking and your heater. First, however, it is important to see how much hot water you use now (on the average) for particular tasks:

tub bath	10 to 15 gallons;
shower	8 to 12 gallons;
baby bath	5 to 7 gallons;
meal preparation	3 to 5 gallons;
dishwashing by hand	3 to 5 gallons;
dishwashing in machine	8 to 14 gallons;
clothes washing	10 to 18 gallons.

As you see, the amount of water for which you must maintain high temperatures is not substantial. There are booster heaters on the market which can be installed for specialized areas where higher temperatures are required rather than supplying the whole system with superheated water continually, at terrific expense.

Another alternative is to install a small water heater where you need temperatures of 150 degrees such as in the kitchen or laundry room. Because a dishwasher uses hot water specifically, you can cut energy costs by installing a small water heater under the sink or in a closet. You can switch it on about half an hour before you need to use your appliance. (You are, at the same time, saving money by getting rid of expensive hot water piping.) The same goes for the laundry room. Meanwhile, you are able to maintain the central water heater at a temperature of only 120 degrees for general use.

Sizing a Water Heater

Sizing is often a problem either for a replacement unit or a unit for a new house. There is really little mystery involved. If you live alone you do not need a 60 or 80 gallon water heater. In fact, you would continually maintain a vast quantity of hot water for little reason. On the other hand, if you have a large family, dishwasher and clothes washer, an undersized unit can often be a nightmare. The table here gives you the gallon storage capacity you probably require—always depending on your particular situation or lifestyle and/or special family members.

HOW TO IMPROVE YOUR HOT WATER SYSTEM

There are other ways in which you can improve your hot water system to reduce energy consumption while still producing an equal or superior hot water supply.

First, install hot and cold mixing valves and automatic shut-off faucets where possible. On showers, new water-saving devices which reduce the flow by 50 percent while still offering a good shower, can be installed. Next, eliminate long piping runs wherever possible. If a faucet has about 40 or 50 feet of pipe between it and the heater, you pull 40 or 50 feet of hot water into the pipe before you get the use of any heated water. When you shut the faucet off, there is still a large quantity of heated water in that pipe which will be wasted. For long runs, as we have already suggested, install a small water heater at the point of use. And of course all pipes which carry hot water and pass through uninsulated areas must be insulated. An insulation that you wrap around pipes is available at local building supply outlets for a few dollars; simply wrap it around pipes and fasten in place. (It's sometimes referred to as heating tape.)

Put in time clocks to turn your water heater on and off. Usually available for under $20, these units shut the water heater off when hot water is not normally needed (during the night) and turn it on again at specified times when needed. By keeping the water heater turned on (and most people do) all night, there is heat loss and the unit must switch on every so often to maintain the temperature. Another way to improve the efficiency and lower the cost of the system, is to switch it off when you will be away from home for a few days or weeks. Most homeowners are unfamiliar with the water heater and fear to tamper with it. But if you look at yours, you will see it is a very simple mechanism. Electric water heaters can be turned "off" and "on" easily. A gas heated system can be switched to the "pilot" position if you want to avoid relighting it on your return. Either way, you save money.

It almost goes without saying that leaky faucets must be fixed! A hot water faucet which only needs a 10¢ washer, can wash away hundreds of gallons of heated water in a short period of time.

Maintenance Tips

The hot water heater doesn't have any moving parts and can go on for years and years with little or no trouble. Most have a good guarantee and warranty behind them which lasts about 5 years. Nevertheless, you should give your hot water heater some attention along with the rest of the hot water system if you want to cut energy bills.

(1) Check, adjust and clean all burners in water heaters. Be sure all heat transfer surfaces are clean.
(2) Drain hot water heater several times a year to remove sediment at the bottom. Sometimes only a pail or two of water removal is necessary.

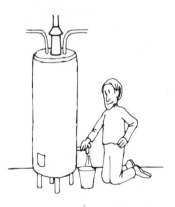

(3) Check and repair all leaky faucets.
(4) Inspect pipes closely. Repair drippy ones and repair or replace insulation wherever required.
(5) Check all thermostats, valves, etc. for proper calibration and operation.

SUGGESTED WATER HEATER SIZING GUIDE
(Gallon Storage Capacity)

House Specification	Number in Family					
	1	2	3	4	5	6
A. One Bath	40	40	40	40	50	50
1—One bath with dishwasher	40	40	40	40	50	50
2—One bath with clothes washer	40	40	40	40	50	50
3—One bath with clothes washer & dishwasher	40	40	40	40	50	50
B. Two Baths	40	40	40	40	50	50
1—Two baths with dishwasher	40	40	40	40	50	50
2—Two baths with clothes washer	40	40	40	40	50	50
3—Two baths with clothes washer & dishwasher	40	40	50	50	50	60
C. Three Baths	40	40	40	40	50	50
1—Three baths with dishwasher	40	40	40	40	50	50
2—Three baths with clothes washer	40	40	50	50	50	60
3—Three baths with clothes washer & dishwasher	40	40	50	60	60	80

8. Complementary Heating Sources

Another way to cut your overall energy bill is to install and use a complementary heat source. This could help offset the high cost of running your central system and could also act as a back-up in case of a power emergency; a real power emergency is not that far-fetched. In recent years, for example, newspapers have been riddled with stories of local brown-outs and black-outs, not to mention the almost annual threat from utilities that there is not enough natural gas or oil available to heat all the houses. Furthermore, another oil embargo could—in a relatively short period of time—directly affect your ability to warm your house.

A complementary heating source can be any other system which supplies some but not all of your heating needs (except, perhaps, in an emergency). Power for such a system could be supplied by another fossil fuel, wood, the sun, wind, water or even organic waste. Because wood and the sun's radiation are among the most viable today as complementary heating sources, they will be focussed on in this chapter.

WOOD HEAT

Wood is one of the oldest sources of heat and even today it is among the cheapest and most available types of fuels. Except in high density urban areas, wood can be purchased by the cord from $40 to $80. In many parts of the country, it lies there for the taking. Perhaps around your own house there are felled trees available for firewood. On virtually any roadway you can find large trees cut up in sections—the highway department's work. A single telephone call to the highway department could furnish you with all your wood needs for one or even several winters. The "harder" the wood (birch, maple) the slower it burns and the more even the heat it projects. The "softer" woods, such as pine, burn quickly in fits and starts. Hard woods usually cost more. You should also beware of buying "green" or unseasoned wet wood; it is extremely hard to burn and gives off quantities of smoke.

The most common way to burn wood, as everyone knows, is in the fireplace. What everyone doesn't know, however, is that many fireplaces are not particularly effective as a complementary heating source. Many fireplaces can add atmosphere to a room or even take the chill out of the house in the spring or autumn, but beyond this the unit is not very effective. Those who use the fireplace during the cold winter days or nights, thinking they are helping to ease the burden on the central heating system, usually wind up doing more harm than good. In nine cases out of ten, the typical fireplace puts an increased strain on the heating system.

This is because most fireplaces are not more than 15 percent efficient. That is, for every log you burn, you receive about 15 percent of the potential heat from it. A lot of the combustible material in wood is lost as a gas to the outside without burning. Also, although the fireplace is not efficient, most fireplace flues are. A good flue will not only draw smoke and products of combustion to the outside but will also draw out about 20 percent of the already heated (and paid for) air of the house, every hour!

Many modern fireplaces come with a door made of a steel grate and fire-resistant glass. This unit has cabinets finished in black porcelain, (2) louvered top for quick heat dissipation, (3) 2-inch thick refractory hearth, (4) 12-gauge steel heavy duty arc-welded combustion chamber, (5) draft control to restrict burning rate and loss of room air, (6) option fan to improve circulation, and (7) glass door (photo courtesy of Martin Industries).

More Efficiency

There are, however, some steps you can take to make your present fireplace more efficient. The damper, which opens and closes the flue, is the place to begin. The damper must *always* be closed when your heating or air conditioning is operating. Even when a fire is not burning, the damper will draw a considerable amount of heated or cooled air from the house. Of course, when you are using natural ventilation to cool your house, an open fireplace damper can be of some help.

Virtually all modern and many old fireplaces come with a damper. *If you do not have a damper on your unit, get one.* For a free-standing fireplace a damper can be purchased for about $25, and easily installed. For older masonry units, the installation is more difficult. This often is not a do-it-yourself project. Until your damper is installed you can temporarily stuff rags or newspapers into the cavity to block off the unwanted air flow. For safety purposes this should only be a temporary measure (make sure the rags are not oily or combustible) and you should make sure that this flue is clear before starting a fire.

Another way to make a fireplace more efficient is to place a cover over the opening to prevent costly heated room air from being lost up the flue. There are basically two types of covers which can be used. Many manufacturers offer a cover which can be put in place while the fire is being enjoyed. This cover is usually made of a steel grate with fire-resistant glass. It enables you to view the fire and receive radiated heat through the glass while substantially reducing the amount of heated room air lost up the flue.

The second type of cover which can be used economically is one that's placed over the fireplace opening at the end of the evening. At this time the fire is usually burning low but you cannot close the damper because there is still smoke going up the flue. While you sleep, the fire eventually dies and the open damper then draws heated air up the chimney instead of smoke. But it's fairly easy to make a cover for both masonry fireplaces with rectangular openings and for free-standing fireplaces.

For the masonry fireplace, simply measure the opening you wish to enclose and then cut a cover from a fire-resistant material such as sheet metal. Do not use plywood—it could ignite. Make sure you measure carefully so that no air drafts can come in around the edges.

It is somewhat more difficult to make a cover for a free-standing unit, especially one with a curved opening. But it is not impossible. Remove the curved screen from your free-standing unit. Place a large piece of paper directly against the screen. Then carefully trace the screen on the paper. Cut along the traced line and you will have a pattern for making the cover. Place this pattern on a piece of sheet metal and mark off the shape. With either

A wide variety of traditional and free-standing fireplaces are available today, and you should be able to make a cover for any of them (courtesy of Fasco Industries, Inc.).

tin snips or a saw, cut out the sheet metal to shape. Then bend the metal to the same shape as the screen.

Wood-Burning Stoves

A much more efficient way to burn wood is in a wood-burning stove. The most efficient types of stoves allow sufficient air for combustion to enter the unit, but no more than that. Besides heating by radiation (as does a fireplace) a wood-burning stove heats by convection and conduction. That is, the entire surface of the unit heats up to warm the air in the room.

There are old-fashioned wood-burning stoves called Franklin stoves that are both very efficient and very beautiful. When the door of the unit is closed, air is drawn from the base of the stove. Some of this is used for combustion. The rest of the air passes over the surface and is heated. These units can still be purchased at prices ranging from $75 to $500, and up. One source for an old stove is either a back country shop or perhaps an antique store. But most manufacturers of fireplaces today produce versions of old stoves such as the Franklin, that are extremely popular, or even an updated version. Although some units may exhibit the original characteristics of the older stoves, they are actually a hybrid between the old stoves and a modern free-standing fireplace.

You can choose between old and new versions of wood-burning stoves. Often antique wood-burning stoves can be purchased in out-of-the-way places for a reasonable price. Manufacturers of fireplaces and stoves are also offering some ''vintage'' models such as the Franklin stove (photo courtesy of United States Stove Co.).

Highly functional wood burning circulator stoves are also available. Although they lack the same grace and beauty of the old stove, they can go a long way in furnishing complementary heat at low cost (photo courtesy of United States Stove Co.).

The closer the unit is to the older stove design, the more efficient. With a good wood-burning stove, there is little draft because no more air is allowed into the unit than is necessary for combustion. Furthermore, logs will burn two or three times longer than in a fireplace and still give you more heat. For instance, a good stove can be filled with wood at bedtime and with the air inlet turned low it will give off heat for ten or twelve hours. This means that if you have a good cheap source of wood, you can keep the stove operating most of the winter and take a substantial chunk out of your heating bill. Many types will save you more money if they have cooking facilities you can use instead of your electric or gas stove.

As mentioned above, a good wood-burning stove costs money. Some discount-type stores offer a version of them for less, but don't be fooled. There are two very important considerations when purchasing such a unit. The stove should be of a heavy gauge steel; the heavier the stove the more it can heat up, and the longer it will last. Secondly, the unit will probably be welded together. A good weld should be smooth (beware of bumps) and there should be no hairline cracks where the weld joins the steel. If the unit you are looking at is painted, check the inside of the unit to see what kind of welding job has been done.

There are fixtures on the market today for about $50 which allow you to make a wood-burning stove out of a 55-gallon drum. These units are handsome and functional. But the 55-gallon drum you obtain should be of a heavy gauge metal. Many drums are made from thin steel and will not hold up very long under the intense heat which is produced. If you decide to make such a stove, before you cut any of the metal (either with a torch or a mechanical saw) check to see that the previous contents of the drum were not combustible. If the drum had been filled with a flammable liquid, fill it with water first to flush it out. Repeat until you are sure the drum is clean.

There are many products on the market today which can help you save valuable energy dollars on primary and complementary heating systems. Some manufacturers are selling a heat circulator which fits into the flue and cycles air which would normally be lost up the chimney, available for between $100 and $150 (photo courtesy of Calcinator Corp.).

Installation Tips

Free-standing fireplaces and wood-burning stoves are installed similarly. Both are quite simple, and if you can handle the unit yourself you can probably do the entire job alone. Depending on how you wish to tackle the project, a new fireplace or wood-burning stove can be located so that the old chimney is used as a flue. Although this is the quickest way to install a new unit, it is not always the best-looking. There are, however, many ways to install stove or fireplace chimneys.

Because there is a fire hazard involved if the unit is not installed properly, we will not detail the entire installation but rather defer to the specific instructions supplied by your particular fireplace or stove manufacturer. Directions vary according to the unit purchased.

A nice touch for free-standing units is to create a surface of slate, brick or even gravel on the floor. Another idea to keep in mind is that stove pipes and chimneys can be directed out through a wall and up the side of the house, or they can exit through the ceiling; but *it is recommended that you direct your pipe through the ceiling.* For an in-depth review of proper selection, care and maintenance of wood-burning stoves and fireplaces, see *Book of Successful Fireplaces.*

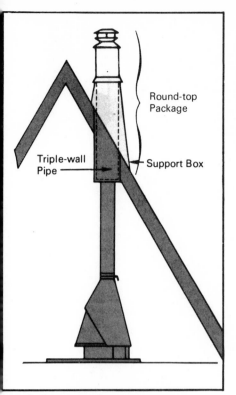

A-frame roofs pose no installation problems with the proper chimney package.

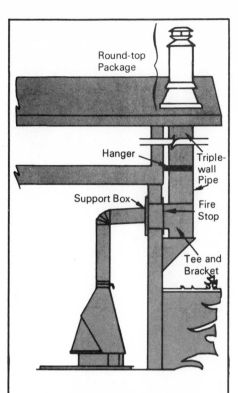

No need to cut through the attic. It's easy to elbow through an outside wall and vent straight up, using Tee and Bracket.

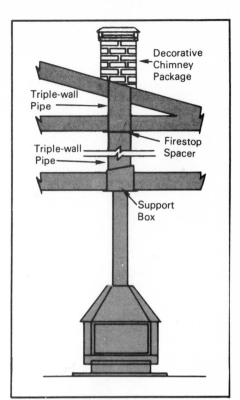

First floor installation in a two-story house. Chimney can be concealed in a second story closet.

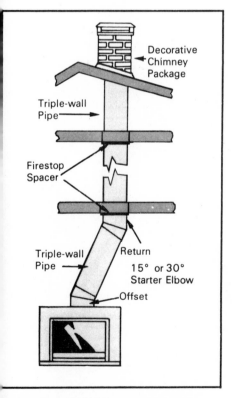

Preway chimneys clear upstairs obstructions with 15° or 30° elbows (all elbow kits include offset and return).

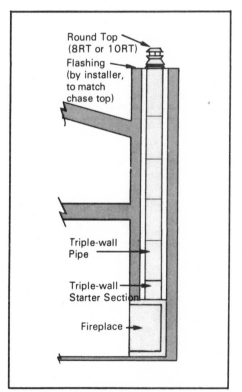

Today's space saving chase installations are a natural with Preway built-in fireplaces and chimney system.

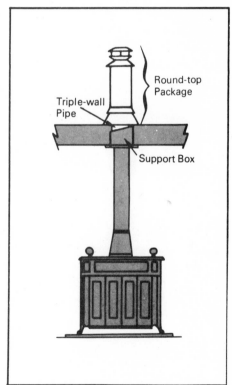

Installation through a flat roof is simple and the most economical of all.

Both fireplaces and wood burning stoves can be installed in a variety of ways: The six Illustrations here detail some typical methods of chimney installation (photo courtesy of Preway).

93

An easy way to install a new stove is to use your old fireplace flue. The entrance of the fireplace can be blocked off; then either use the old flue or install new piping up through the chimney (photo courtesy of Department of Agriculture).

SOLAR HEAT

Solar energy systems are quickly gaining popularity both as primary and complementary heating sources. Only a few years ago these systems were considered a thing of the future. Today, there are a variety of products and systems on the market which you can use to complement your present heating system.

There are important advantages and disadvantages to current systems and the state of the technology in general. The sun obviously is a large and continuing source of free energy. Its heat is widely distributed and its use as a fuel does not alter the earth's overall heat inventory. But there are disadvantages: sunlight provides a relatively low energy source in comparison to the energy obtained from fossil fuels; also, the form of energy is intermittent and variable due to daily, seasonal and environmental effects. The real challenge, therefore, is to create a complementary energy system which can either use the energy when it is available or use the energy in conjunction with a storage system.

Collecting Solar Energy

The sun heats the earth by radiation similar to a fireplace heating a room. Any surface that the sun's rays touch, heats up. When the surface heats up to a temperature greater than objects surrounding it, the surface begins to lose heat by conduction, convection and re-radiation.

Solar collectors in common use today have a transparent cover of glass or another material which allows the sun's rays to enter but not escape. Under this cover, a medium such as water or alcohol absorbs this heat. A transporter system, usually metal pipes, moves this heat to where it will either be used or stored. So long as these three items are present, a solar collector can be made of various materials to fit different purposes. In many systems the heat gained from the solar collectors is stored in a large tank in the cellar until needed.

The key problem with solar energy systems today is that they are expensive (and also not available in stores). And until equipment is either mass-produced or some other breakthrough cuts the price, it will remain expensive. Most systems, for a relatively small house, will cost between $3,000 and $5,000. Such a system would supply about 30 to 40 percent of the annual heat required.

There are other systems available that supply energy for heating water for baths and other home uses. Some solar collectors are being used to heat swimming pools. Given the current state of solar energy technology, it is a viable but still expensive way to help heat your home. Although not displayed in stores, you can find out about a solar system for your home by writing to the various companies listed in the directory at the back of the book.

OTHER HEAT SOURCES

There is work being done today to tap virtually every type of power source available. Many people have successfully erected wind mills, with an electric generator tied into batteries to furnish power for the home. If the prevailing winds are right, such a system can provide plenty of "free" power. The problem is, again, that the system itself costs a lot of money. A good wind-generating system costs upward of $5,000.

Where a good source of running water is available it is still possible to build a mill, again tied into a generator and batteries for a constant source of electrical energy. As above, this system is quite expensive. Some people are also experimenting with methane generators that tap decaying organic matter for energy. Such systems are usually beyond the scope or interest of a homeowner who is looking for a simple way to complement his or her current heating system.

Solar collectors are flat, darkened plates exposed under glass to the sun's rays. On this house the collectors have been built into the steep southern roof...

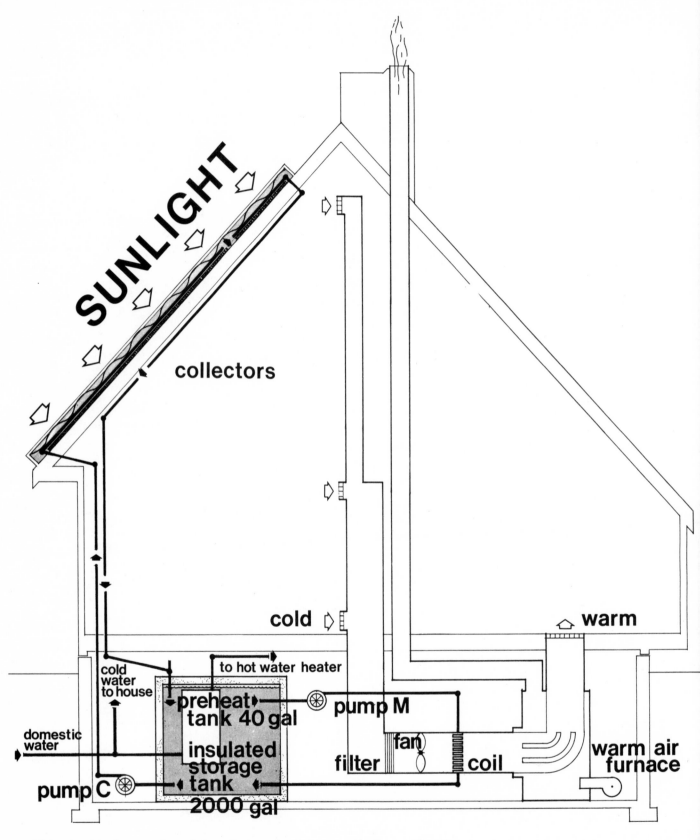

SUNLIGHT

collectors

cold

warm

to hot water heater

cold
water
to house

preheat
tank 40 gal

pump M

domestic
water

insulated
storage
tank
2000 gal

pump C

filter

fan

coil

warm air
furnace

Water circulates by pump through the collectors where it is warmed by the sun. Then the fluid is moved to a 2,400-gallon tank beneath the house where heat is stored.

When heat is needed by house, a second pump transfers heat from storage tank to air (drawings courtesy of Acorn Structures, Inc.).

9. Creating New Living Space

Every time you add more living area to your home, you increase the heating and cooling load. It would pay, therefore, to place energy conservation on an equal footing with design elements and aesthetic appeal when planning either a room addition or a remodeling project. A properly planned and executed project will help you hold any increase in energy bills to a minimum. With some projects, you may even be able to cut the monthly bill down.

By planning energy conservation into an added unit, the full-cost increase can be held to a minimum or in some cases actually be lowered (M.J. Sweet).

Considerable energy dollars can be saved on all home improvement projects by employing the ideas detailed in earlier sections of this book. The following specialized techniques will save you still more.

SHOULD YOU "CONVERT" OR "ADD" SPACE?

On a typical project there is more of a savings on energy and materials in a conversion that in an addition. The reason is simple. On a conversion of unused space, the roof above and the foundation below are already in place. The most popular types of conversions include: the attic, basement, attached garage, breezeway, or unfinished room.

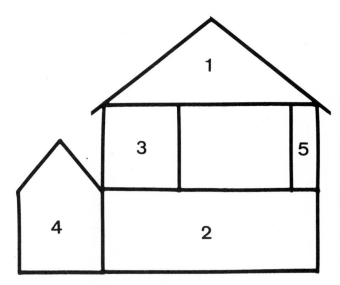

Converting wasted interior space is usually less expensive and more energy efficient than adding either a room extension or addition. Some of the more popular areas to convert are: (1) attic; (2) basement; (3) unfinished room; (4) attached garage; (5) breezeway.

On an addition where a roof and foundation must be installed, the room extensions will usually mean adding to your energy bills at the same time. Obviously whichever route you decide to take depends on unused space available in the home, what you wish to achieve through the expansion, your plot plan, and many other items.

To help you decide which way to go, here are a few rough dollar estimates for various jobs. If you live in a one-story bungalow, you can convert it to a two-story house by adding a double dormer on the second level. Many people who purchased a basic tract house during the early 1950's used this method to almost double their living space. The basic structure plus windows will cost you between $6,000 and $7,000. If you wish to add a bathroom to the area, it will cost between $1,600 and $2,000 extra. All finishes and insulation will be extra. (These figures are based on using a contractor who provides all the materials.)

If your attic is suitable for conversion and can be finished off without major structural change, the cost will run from $1,500 to $2,000. If a single dormer or more windows need to be added, the price tag will jump to a minimum of $3,000.

A basement can be economically converted into usable living space for $1,500 to $2,000. Depending on what you wish to do with this area, the price can, of course, be much higher.

You can usually plan that for an addition or extension to the home, the cost usually runs between $24 and $35 per square foot. So if you wish to add a 15- by 25-foot living room, you will gain approximately 375 square feet of space. Be prepared, however, to spend between $9,000 and $13,000. Adding specialized areas, such as kitchens, can raise this figure.

These are ballpark figures. Depending on how much of the actual work you do, the contractor you hire, the cost of materials in your part of the country, and the type of room you plan, the price will be higher or lower.

Room additions usually cost about $25 to $35 per square foot of space, but for specialized rooms such as bathrooms or kitchens, the cost can run considerably higher (M.J. Sweet).

Basements can be converted for about $1,500 and $2,000 depending on how extensive the work. Above, wasted space is turned into a comfortable family area (U.S. Plywood).

CONVERTING INTERIOR SPACE

Since it is usually cheaper to convert space which already exists, the attic can be a very profitable area even if the present space lacks adequate insulation. By adding insulation directly between the roof rafters and to the end walls, and then finishing the room with sheetrock, not only will you have more living space, but an energy-efficient attic as well. With such a conversion, you can probably save between $100 and $200 or more on your energy bill.

The basement is another choice for conversion from an energy-efficiency standpoint. When the masonry walls of the basement are insulated (see Chapter 1 for details) and rigid insulation is placed around the outside perimeter of the footings, this room can be made comfortable and weathertight. Often the heat from the furnace and hot water heater will be sufficient to keep this space warm without having to add more heating ducts. Where it is not sufficient, a small wood-burning stove or perhaps several small low wattage electric wall heaters can be added.

Attached garages have become popular for conversion, often lowering energy bills. By insulating and finishing the walls in this area, heat loss from the wall of the house is greatly reduced. This is particularly true if the garage is located on the north side in cold climates and the south or east side in warm climates. (If you are having car-ignition problems during cold weather, there are low-energy devices which can be purchased at auto sup-

Where natural light is a problem, an interior space can be made enjoyable with special-area lighting (U.S. Plywood).

ply houses to help you start your car in cold weather. One such device is an oil dip-stick heater, which keeps the car's oil warm so that it can be started more easily on cold mornings.)

ENERGY-SAVING WAYS TO EXPAND YOUR HOME

The following sections give tips which you can apply when adding space through either conversion or addition. Regardless of what type of expansion project you plan, study the following ideas to find those you can use.

Orienting Space

Although your house layout or property lines may dictate where you can expand, some space uses should be directed toward the sun and others away from it.

Additional Room	SUGGESTED ORIENTATION			
	North	South	East	West
Bedroom	3	1	1	4
Living Room	4	1	2	1
Dining Room	4	1	1	2
Kitchen	4	1	1	4
Bathroom	1	1	1	1
Garage (cold climate)	1	4	3	3
Garage (warm climate)	4	1	2	2
Laundry Room	1	4	2	2
Playroom	4	1	1	3

Table above offers suggested orientations for particular rooms when adding space: (1) excellent; (2) good; (3) fair; (4) poor.

Bedrooms. The bedroom should be placed on the east or south side of the house for maximum benefits and minimum energy consumption. In the winter, the early morning sun will help heat this room. In summer, this early morning sun will not overly heat the room until after the occupant or occupants have left. This exposure helps with summer cooling. Although the sun may shine in all morning, by bedtime this section of the house has been in the shade for many hours and has had time to cool off. Whenever possible, avoid placing the bedroom on the west side of the house where the afternoon sun can heat the room to uncomfortable temperatures, requiring air conditioning to cool it before bedtime.

Living room. This room, especially if it is used actively during the day, should be located on the east or south to take advantage of solar heating during the winter. If proper shading is used the sun won't interfere with summer activities, while in the evening the living room will be cool.

Dining room. Although the dining room could be located on the south or east side of the house, it also can be located in the west. If it is used for most evening meals, the western exposure might help heat it in the winter (but watch out for glare from the setting sun). Obviously, a problem could arise with summer overheating. There are two ways to overcome this: (1) deciduous trees could be planted on the west side of the house or (2) an eating deck could be built right off the dining room. This eating deck will allow you to enjoy the evening summer breezes when the dining room gets overheated.

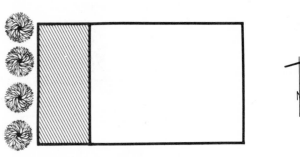

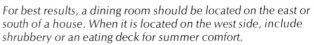

For best results, a dining room should be located on the east or south of a house. When it is located on the west side, include shrubbery or an eating deck for summer comfort.

Kitchen. A major activity area in most homes, this room should get an eastern or southern exposure to utilize natural sunlight without overheating.

Bathroom. This room can be successfully placed in any location because it is used for relatively short intervals. You should therefore consider the more critical factor of how far your hot water pipes would be from the main hot water source.

Garage. In cold climates place it on the north side of the house, as a wind break to prevent heat loss. In hot climates place it on the south or west side to block heat gain into the house. In mild climates it can be placed on either side.

Laundry room. This is another room which can be placed in any direction because it is used for relatively short intervals. (But again, keep in mind those hot water pipes and the distance they must run from the hot water source to the planned area.) Often the north wall is preferable. Because the appliances create their own heat for this space, cold weather is not a problem. By placing it on the north side you can avoid summer overheating, since the sun will not add to the heat buildup. (Look closely at chapters dealing with hot water, venting, insulation, and appliances.)

Playroom. There are several choices for placement of this room, which sees an unusual amount of activity. It can be located on the east, south or west side of a home where sunlight and warmth (without overheating) are obtained. The northern exposure (dark and cold) should be avoided.

Other specialized rooms should be located similarly as above. For example, if an older person lives in the house located in the southern part of the U.S., his or her bedroom/study should be situated to take advantage of early morning sun but should be shielded from late afternoon sun, particularly in the summer. In the north, the opposite holds true. If possible, the library or home workshop should be located to take greatest advantage of solar heating and light.

Garages and Carports. Finishing off these areas into living space can help to reduce your energy bills by lowering energy consumption. In cold climates place the garage on the north, northeast or northwest exposure to serve as a buffer against cold winds. In hot climates, put the attached garage or carport on the east or west walls to help cut down on heat buildup.

Windows. See chapter 2 for details of creating better windows both in your present home and new construction. It is sufficient to say here that when converting or adding space, use double-glazed windows whenever possible. If you must use single-pane glass, be sure to add a storm window to cut energy loss. Even in hot climates, this double thickness of glass will help reduce heat gain by conduction.

Window location is another matter which requires careful consideration. Just as you should locate your addition carefully, so should you place windows with care. In the summer the sun's rays are the most intense on the east and west side. In the winter the sun is most intense on the south side. To gain needed heat in the winter and avoid it in the summer, orient as many windows as possible to the south. Of course, you must abide by your local building code and the building department may have something to say about how much glass you put where. When large

quantities of glass are used in east and west, you might consider tinted or reflective glass. As mentioned earlier, you can work around this problem at low cost by trees and other shading devices.

Shade. As detailed in Chapter 2, shades and blinds can be used to reduce heat buildup in the summer due to radiation and conduction. When adding space to your home, plan on adding trees for shade. Deciduous- or leaf-bearing trees can be placed on the east, south and west sides of the home. This type of vegetation allows the sun's light through in the winter but blocks it out in the summer. Evergreen or coniferous trees can be successfully placed on the north side of the house. Because these trees are green all year 'round, they will act as a wind break in the winter. Avoid placing them on the south side of the house, however, as they will tend to block the sun out in the winter when you need it most. Plan on a roof overhang to cut heat gain in summer.

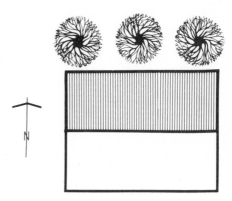

Plant evergreens on additions facing north. This acts as a windbreak in the winter (Owens-Corning Fiberglas).

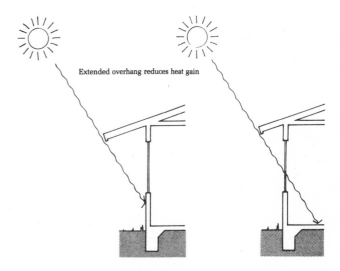

One way to block the sun's rays from a room addition is to plan a roof overhang which will let in the sun during the winter but not during the summer (Owens-Corning Fiberglas).

Shape of Space

When building an addition or extension, it should be as close to a square as possible to cut down on heat loss through walls and roof. Long narrow additions or extensions should be avoided if serious energy conservation is important.

Ceiling Height. Spaces with high ceilings require much more heat and air conditioning to keep the area comfortable. In a room with a standard height ceiling, you will conserve energy by reducing it from 8 feet to 7½ feet. Keep this in mind when tempted to raise the height of an attic ceiling at the centerpoint.

Doors

Exterior doors are responsible for considerable heat gain and loss. When planning a new addition, purchase one of the new insulated doors on the market. These cut heat gain and loss through the material. Of course, when doors are installed, special care should be taken when applying weather stripping to reduce air infiltration.

A good way to greatly reduce air infiltration either on a new addition or in your home as it now stands would be to add a vestibule between your exterior and the outside. Or, you may want to investigate creating an entry or foyer on the inside of your home. Both kinds of entries would act as a buffer between the air outdoors and your heated or cooled house air. This is relatively inexpensive to build and will mean a big saving when the heating system or air conditioner is running.

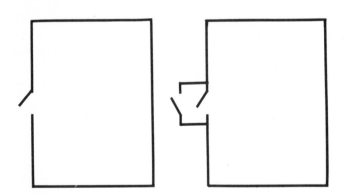

A vestibule can be added to a house with little problem.

Sliding glass doors should never be used for just a view or light—a well-insulated and installed window is considerably more energy efficient. When a sliding glass door is called for in an addition or conversion, make sure it is the thermal-break type with double-glazed glass. Properly installed and weather stripped, these units are more efficient than the typical sliding glass door.

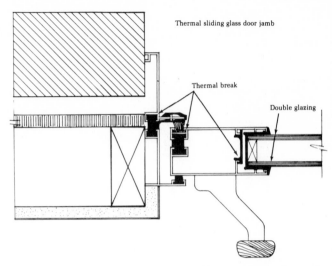

When a sliding glass door is used, make sure it has the thermal-break type, double-glazed door. Properly weather stripped and installed, they are much more energy efficient than typical sliding glass doors (Owens-Corning Fiberglas).

Grading

Water is never beneficial around a house. When siting a new addition or extension, try to do it so that the final grade of land can be sloped away from the construction. The dryer you can keep the earth around your home, the warmer it will be, thus cutting down on heat loss.

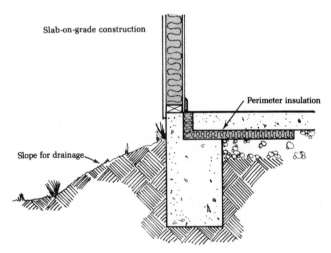

Slab should be insulated as shown in diagram. When planning final grading around your addition, have ground slope away from unit to keep area dryer (Owens-Corning Fiberglas).

Insulation

If you are constructing a project which is slab on grade, insulate around the slab to about 24 inches inward.

As detailed in Chapter 1, all crawl spaces must be insulated to prevent energy loss through the floor. This applies to your present house as well as new construction.

In your present house, chances are your walls are constructed of 2 x 4 inch framing members. For your new project use 2 x 6 inch framing members. This will allow you to put thicker insulation into the cavities, thus cutting down on heat gain and loss. If codes permit, place wall studs 24 inches o.c.

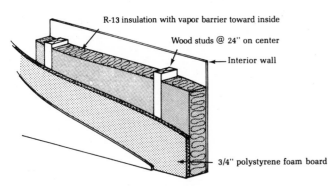

If possible on new construction, space wall studs 24 inches apart (Owens-Corning Fiberglas).

For any interior conversion or new addition, the roof must be insulated to the fullest extent possible. Many homes are constructed with 2 by 8 inch roof rafters. If this is the case in your house, add a full 8 inches of insulation. For new additions, again insulate fully (see Chapter 1 for more details).

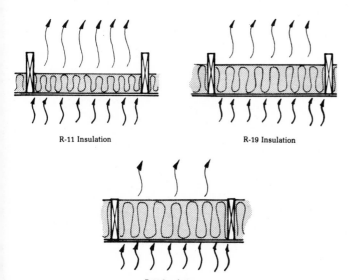

The larger the R-factor, the greater it will retard heat flow

Insulate roof to maximum. The more insulation you add, the lower the heat gain or loss (Owens-Corning Fiberglas).

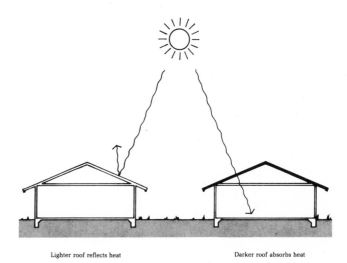

Select light-colored roof shingles to reflect sun and dark colors to absorb it (Owens-Corning Fiberglas).

Roofing

Light-colored shingles tend to reflect the sun's heat while dark shingles absorb it. For new additions, use shingles which are dark in cold climates and light-colored shingles in warm climates. When it comes time to re-do your roof, select a color for your roof suitable to your area's climate.

Quality Control

Any job must be done well to keep energy bills to a minimum. If you do all the work yourself, by reading this and earlier chapters in the book you will be aware of how to achieve "tight" construction. Even if you have a contractor do all of the work, you or your architect should inspect the job frequently to assure good quality. This means that all cracks must be caulked. All "little spaces" around windows and light switches must be stuffed with insulation. All windows and doors must be weather stripped, plus all the many other items detailed in earlier chapters.

Air Infiltration

A project which you undertake and which includes doors, windows, pipes to the outside faucet, etc., will have to be fully caulked (see Chapter 2 for how-to details). Whether you do the work yourself or have a contractor do it, you should first check what needs caulking and then make sure these areas are done.

Heating and Cooling

Try to incorporate your present heating and cooling system to heat and cool the new living space. If the new area

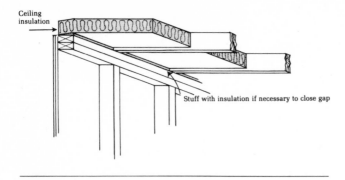

Ceiling insulation

Stuff with insulation if necessary to close gap

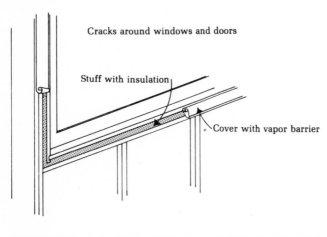

Cracks around windows and doors

Stuff with insulation

Cover with vapor barrier

Insulate behind pipes and electrical boxes

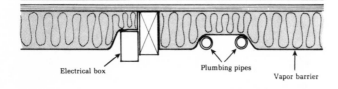

Electrical box

Plumbing pipes

Vapor barrier

is not used constantly, perhaps a wood-burning stove will suffice, or several small electric heaters. When new heating and cooling is needed for an extensive project, try not to oversize the equipment. When applying all of the other energy tips listed above, you can usually get away with a smaller unit than what might otherwise be used in a typically constructed project. Be sure to question your architect and heating/cooling contractor on this point. They usually specify a larger piece of equipment than needed to include a "safety factor." If your project is energy efficient in all other ways, often the "safety factor" will be unnecessary.

Ventilation

Ventilation will help keep your new area cool in the summer and dry in the winter. For a small addition, often windows oriented to achieve cross-ventilation will be sufficient. When a sloping roof is involved, small static vents at the top of the ceiling will greatly reduce heat buildup. When converting an attic, do not cover up any ventilators already in place. When considering an attic conversion and the room is hot even at night during the summer months, deal with this problem as in Chapter 4. Or, as a viable alternative to adding air conditioning, consider attic fans (discussed in Chapter 3).

Despite all energy conservation measures designed into new expansion project, without careful quality control they are for naught. These details show three areas to check for proper insulation.

10. Special Energy-Saving Homes

On reading earlier sections of this book, you may have discovered that serious energy conservation (cutting power bills to the core) is neither an art nor a science. In most cases, it is the application of better construction methods, advanced products, and a healthy dose of good horse sense.

Yet if you are thinking of building a new home, you may be wondering how all these very different methods and applications can be pulled together, literally under one roof. Although it is beyond the scope of this chapter to tell you how to actually design and construct an energy-conservation home, it will give you an overview so that you can make more informed decisions. We will here discuss recently designed or constructed energy conservation homes. Not every system or method will fit your budget or climate but they will help you decide what items you want in your new home or addition to make it more energy efficient.

Energy-conservation house uses roof overhangs and protected entryways to reduce heat gain and loss. Because this house was constructed in the warm California climate, light-colored walls and roof were used to help reflect sun (Family Circle Magazine/American Plywood Association).

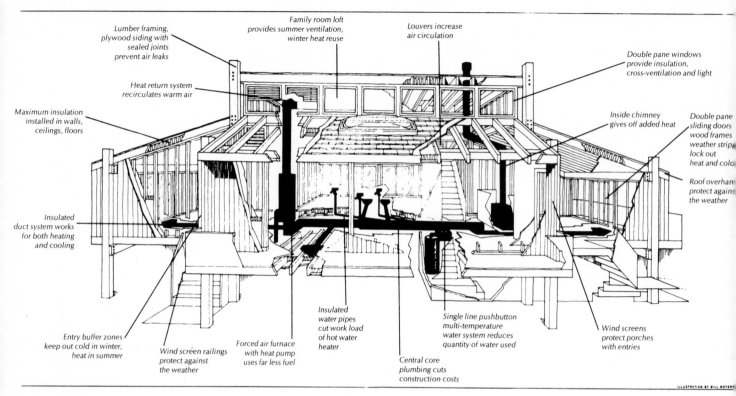

Illustration details many energy-conserving features that can be applied to your home for big energy and dollar savings (Family Circle Magazine/American Plywood Association).

FAMILY CIRCLE/APA ENERGY-SAVING HOUSE

Family Circle Magazine and the American Plywood Association cooperated to build a 1,750 square foot, two-story house in San Diego, California. Designed by PBD Architects Associated, San Diego, the unit reportedly cuts overall heating and water bills by one-half compared to typical units in the area. This unit is an excellent example of the input necessary to achieve energy conservation. Many items applied to this home can be designed into your new home for big energy dollar saving.

The basic shape of the house, a heat re-use system which minimizes winter heating requirements, and a natural ventilation system which makes the house independent of mechanical cooling systems, are three of the key factors in cutting energy costs. For summer cooling, this house acts as a well-functioning chimney. Cool air is introduced through windows and doors on the first floor. It is drawn up through the house and exhausted through open windows in the second story loft. In the winter, the same design works in reverse to cut the central heating load. Heat from the sun, the furnace and the fireplace is collected through closed windows in the loft and redistributed throughout the house with the help of a mechanical blower.

The efficient and economical operation of natural and mechanical heating and cooling systems is also reflected in the unit's floor plan. The layout of the house is open with a minimum of interior partitions so that heat and light are permitted to cover larger areas than they would in a house of comparable size with more interior partitions. In addition to providing natural cooling and heating, the design offers all the energy-saving dimensions of a two-story house. Approximately 20 percent of the heat needed to keep a house warm in the winter escapes through the roof. Therefore, a two-story house (which has less overall roof area than a one-story house of comparable square footage) offers a great heat-loss reduction.

All exterior rooms are oriented well; the unit takes full advantage of the sun's energy without sacrificing a handsome appearance. For example, the house is positioned so that the bedroom wings receive the early morning sun while activity areas receive late afternoon sun. In summer, when afternoon and evening activities may be oriented to the outdoor decks and leisure areas around the house, this arrangement gives the bedrooms time to cool off before sleeping hours. In winter, the same arrangement offers maximum natural heat for activity areas in the afternoon and evening.

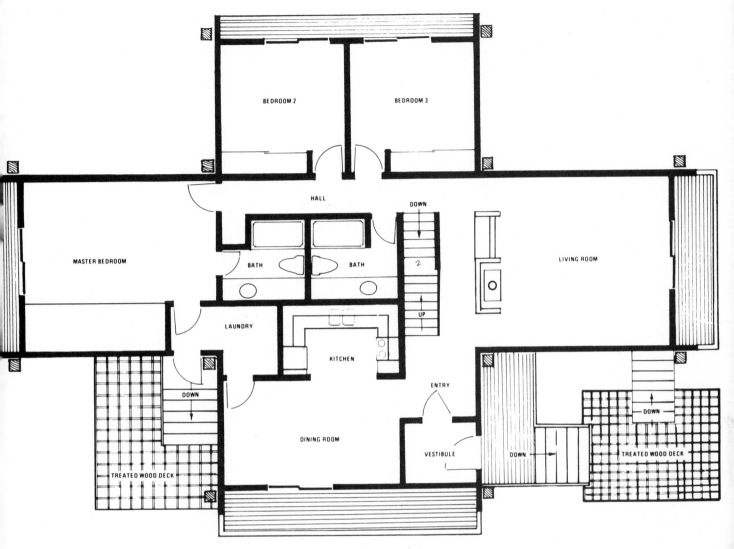

Placement of sleeping and living areas is essential for energy saving. In this unit, bedrooms are placed to get early morning sun while afternoon and evening light shines on activity centers (Family Circle Magazine/American Plywood Association).

Climate control within the house is also assured by the protection of all entries. In addition to exterior wind screens and weather stripped doors, vestibules with inner and outer doors are used to protect entries. These small ante-rooms provide a buffer area or air lock. This reduces the flow of outside air into the house and also prevents the escape of air which has been conditioned.

The house is wood frame construction with plywood panels for the exterior finish. Careful attention was given to the selection and installation of insulation. Fiberglass insulation with a polyethylene vapor barrier to prevent moisture infiltration was used on floors, walls and ceilings. Because the floor is an area of high heat loss, R-19 foil-faced fiberglass insulation was applied between the floor joists. The remainder of the insulation used was unfaced fiberglass, R-11 applied to the walls and R-19

applied to the ceiling. Additional floor insulation was provided with cushion-backed vinyl flooring and carpeting.

The color chosen for the roofing, like the color of exterior walls, is a light neutral. A light color was used on the roof and walls because summer cooling is more of a problem in this geographic area than winter heating. In hot climates the roof should always be a light color. In cold climates, a darker roofing material should be selected. In mild climates, an intermediate color should be the choice.

Roof structure is also important. The shape of the roof structure in this house can adapt to a variety of climates. The roof sections over the living area are pitched. These pitched roofs absorb less heat than flat roofs and provide for high vaulted ceilings that permit heat to rise and be exhausted through the loft. Both these factors aid summer cooling. The nearly flat roof which covers the second story loft also works effectively for conservation of energy, even in areas where both extreme heat and cold are problems. Constructed with a ridge along its perimeter, the flat roof section provides for storage of 2½ inches of water on top of the house. In summer, this water reflects the sunlight and helps keep the house cool. The same loft roof structure works to keep the house warm in winter. In heavy snow regions, the snow remains on top of the nearly flat roof and acts as a natural insulator against the extreme cold.

Windows and glass doors throughout the energy conservation house have double panes of insulated glass separated by ½-inch air space. The units are encased in wood frames that reduce heat and cold transfer. They are weather stripped to prevent air infiltrations and shaded with venetian blinds. Sliding glass doors are wind protected by porches and shaded by roof overhangs. Although the roof overhangs screen out the sun in the summer, they are designed to admit the warm sunlight in winter, when the sun's angle is lower.

Along with the design, materials, and construction systems, the energy-conserving home's mechanical systems are designed to achieve overall economy in operation. The fully insulated duct system takes in hot air which rises to the loft and redistributes it back to the rest of the house. The duct outlets are located around the perimeter of the house, providing heat and counteracting any heat loss through the wall or glass areas. Rather than locating ducts under the house, this home has ducts in the floor panels for protection from heat loss. A gas-fired forced air heating system was also used (gas is still available in this area of the country). The ducts system, however, could be used with heating sources other than gas. The electric pump, for instance, could be used if no gas were available.

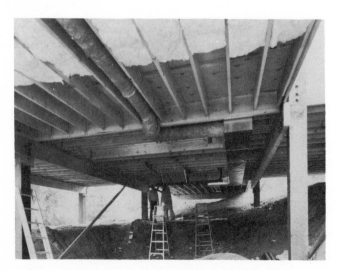

Fully insulated duct system is located within floor panels to cut heat loss (Family Circle Magazine/American Plywood Association).

As for plumbing, water heating and distribution systems were installed in a compact, centrally located core. Besides reducing materials cost and labor, the short pipe runs greatly reduce heat loss common to conventional systems. This central core is located adjacent to a water heater with a temperature of 120 degrees rather than the traditional 140 to 150 setting. The water distribution system complements the central core plumbing. It is a new system which reduces installation costs, water and sewage bills, water heating costs, and maintenance requirements.

Rather than using faucet valves which leak, this system relies on remotely operated low-voltage control to regulate the temperature and flow of water. This system allows the user to preselect temperature and water flow. For example, at the kitchen sink there is a choice of hot, warm, and cold at high and low flow rates. The shower control panel provides three warm temperatures preadjusted by the user. Rather than turning on the faucet and running the water until it reaches the temperature you desire, you simply press a button and immediately receive water which has been heated to your satisfaction.

In the area of lighting, this unit has fluorescent bulbs wherever possible. Wastefully overlighting or underlighting the house (in an effort to economize) is eliminated through the use of the selective lighting scheme. This provides efficient task-oriented lighting throughout the house. Although excessive general lighting is reduced with this plan, adequate lighting is provided in all areas. In the kitchen, for example, fluorescent lights are installed under all overhead cabinets. Positioning these lamps close to the tabletop work surfaces makes it possible to give sufficient lighting using lower wattage bulbs. Track lighting with incandescent bulbs is used in the living and dining areas. The spotlights used in these tracks are low wattage bulbs which concentrate light only in specific areas, where needed. White walls and bright colors used for flooring and tabletops throughout the house expand the use of available light.

Rather than selecting all appliances from one manufacturer, the designers selected the most energy-stingy units available. For example, a 19-cubic foot frost-free refrigerator which uses a Freon-foamed insulation saved 25 to 45 percent of the electricity required by comparative models. The cooking range used, offers a savings from 22 to 25 percent over conventional ranges. The range delivers heat through an induction system—cooking without a flame or hot surface elements. The unit provides heat within the utensils but the range never heats up. The kitchen is also equipped with a microwave oven used as a second oven for cooking. This microwave requires approximately 75 percent less energy than its conventional counterpart. The dishwasher selected has a wash cycle which may be operated independently of the dry cycle.

Low-wattage track lighting on ceiling is used; this task lighting concentrates light on the specific areas where it is needed most (Family Circle Magazine / American Plywood Association).

Unit takes advantage of the natural light and the carefully placed electric lights within house. In kitchen area, fluorescent lighting is installed under all overhead cabinets (Family Circle Magazine/American Plywood Association).

When only the wash cycle is used and dishes are allowed to dry by evaporation, approximately 34 percent of the energy required by the conventional dishwasher is saved.

ARKANSAS ENERGY-SAVING HOUSE

One of the most practical approaches to energy conservation in new construction has resulted from the joint effort of the Arkansas Power & Light Company, a government official, and a heating and air-conditioning wholesaler in Little Rock, Arkansas. To date there have been scores of homes built using this system. Heating and cooling bills have been reduced by 60 percent or more compared to standard homes in the area. What's more, there is a savings on building materials and labor with this system.

One of the key features of the system is the wall framing. In typical wood frame homes wall studs are 2 by 4 inches and placed 16 o.c. This has been a long-time standard throughout the industry. In these new energy-saving homes, wall studs are 2 by 6 inches and are placed 24 inches o.c. This method results in two savings on

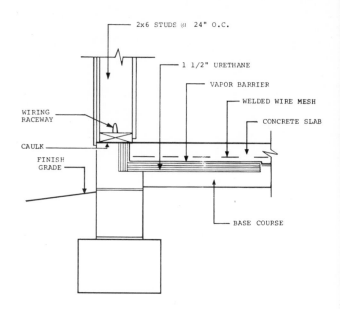

SECTION THRU SLAB

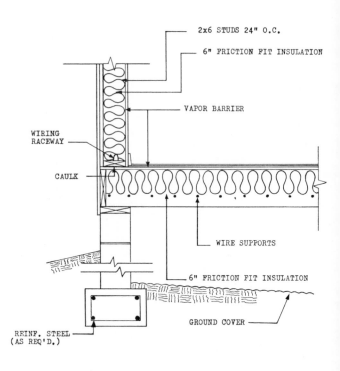

CRAWL SPACE CONSTRUCTION (INSULATION)

With well-insulated walls and ceiling, the obvious place for heat loss is the floor. To prevent this, 6 inches of fiberglass insulation is placed over crawl space. When house is slab-on-grade construction, 1 ½ inches of rigid polyurethane foam insulation is placed around perimeter of slab (Owens-Corning Fiberglas).

energy. Because of the larger space (6 inches versus 4 inches) more insulation can be applied. Further, wood is more heat conductive than is insulation. By placing the studs at a greater distance, there is less wood surface over which to lose heat. A polyethylene vapor barrier completely covers both studs and insulation.

Crawl space and slab have been well insulated in these homes. Although hot air rises, heat also flows from the warmer to the cooler area. Therefore, if the walls and ceiling are well insulated, heat will be lost through the

floor. To combat this energy loss, 6 inches of fiberglass insulation is placed over crawl spaces and a minimum of 1½ inches of rigid polyurethane foam insulation is placed around the perimeter of the slab. Because dampness can chill and require greater use of energy to operate a dehumidifier, the area under the slab is provided with a substantial plastic sheet vapor barrier. Similarly, when a crawl space is used, it must be fully covered with a vapor barrier and the space must also be ventilated with static vents.

DESIGN FEATURES OF THE ARKANSAS ENERGY CONSERVATION HOME
(Illustrative Perspectives)

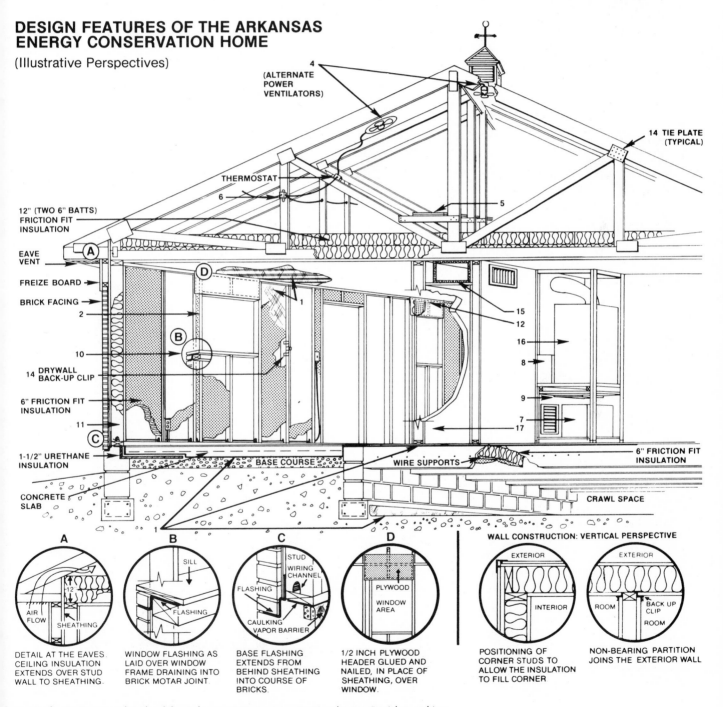

Typical construction details of the Arkansas energy conservation home. Besides seeking to achieve maximum energy conservation in these units, the designers also created a house that's buildable at a very moderate price (Owens-Corning Fiberglas).

Ceilings are fit with 12 inches of Friction Fit fiberglass batt insulation to achieve a value of R-38. As with walls and floor, a complete vapor barrier under the ceiling insulation is specified.

Other specifications of the Arkansas House which help to achieve lower energy bills are:

(1) Vapor Barriers—Walls, ceilings and floors are provided with a positive vapor barrier covering the entire surface of the unit. The use of polyethylene sheeting for vapor barriers is said to be more effective than vapor barriers attached to insulation, because this covers the entire stud area and permits visual inspection of the insulation and vapor barrier before installation of interior wall finish.

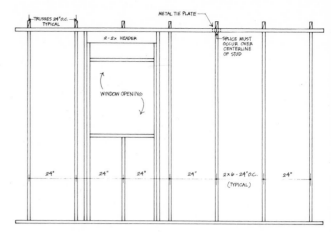

Window area in house does not exceed 8 percent of total floor space. That is, for every 1,000 square feet of floor space there is no more than 80 square feet of glass (Owens-Corning Fiberglas).

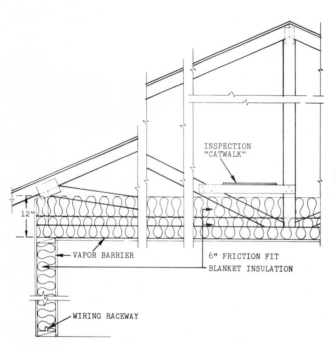

Polyethylene sheeting is used as vapor barrier (Owens-Corning Fiberglas).

(2) Prime windows—All have storm windows and are caulked in place. Window area does not exceed 8 percent of the square footage of the living area. That is, for every 1,000 square feet of living area there can be 80 square feet of window. Overhangs prevent the direct entry of the sun into the unit during the hot season. Also, glass which is exposed to the direct radiation of the sun is fitted with a shading device.

(3) Exterior doors—1¾ inch metal-faced doors have urethane core insulation and magnetic weather stripping.

(4) Attics—Vented with power roof ventilators and with eave vents evenly spaced along the soffits (see

Chapter 4 on ventilation); the net free air equal to 80 square inches per 100 CFM of fan capacity. The power vents are located near the roof ridge and centrally positioned in order to remove hot air throughout the attic space. Ventilators have a capacity to provide not less than 10 air changes per hour. Eighty square feet of soffit vents are provided for every 100 cubic feet of fan capacity. A thermostat controls the power vent switching on at 100 degrees and off at 85 degrees. This temperature range prevents the fan from continually switching on and off.

(5) Wiring and piping is installed so that insulation can be applied correctly. In walls, wiring is allowed to lie on the sill plate by cutting suitable notches in the base of wall studs. In the attic, wiring is attached to or through roof trusses at a point higher than the insulation.

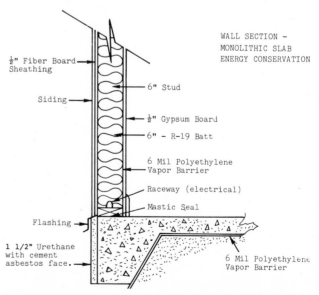

Note that electrical raceway (channel that holds electrical wire) lies on sill plate. This allows electrical wire to be installed in wall without interfering with insulation (Owens-Corning Fiberglas).

(6) For moisture control, a humidifier is used which can provide 50 percent humidity at 70 degrees during the heating season. A dehumidifier capable of maintaining 40 percent humidity at 76 degrees is used for the cooling season.

(7) All heating ducts are insulated with three inches of insulation when passed through any uninsulated areas.

DECADE 80 SOLAR HOUSE

Another method of cutting fuel bills was recently developed by The Copper Development Association. The group built a big 3,400 square foot home in Tucson, Arizona called the Decade 80 Solar House. The goal was to make it as self-sufficient as possible utilizing the sun's energy for heating and cooling the unit. Using solar energy, the house obtains 75 percent of the power needed for cooling; for heating and the operation of electrical appliances, the sun supplies 100 percent of the needed power. Although first costs of this prototype house are high, many of these design elements could become commercially available (and affordable) in the near future.

The roof of the house and the solar panels are interconnected. The panels consist of 2 feet by 8 feet copper sheets, 0.016-inch thick and laminated to plywood. They are combined with rectangular copper tubes to carry water—the energy system's transport and storage medium. The copper panels and copper tubes are blackened to absorb radiant heat more efficiently, transferring this heat to water which circulates throughout the house in copper tubing. On cloudy days when less energy is available from the sun, a buried, insulated tank provides standby energy in the form of 3,000 gallons of solar-heated water.

In addition to the solar collector panels, the house's energy system also incorporates silicon solar cells on the roof. This converts the sun's energy to low voltage power for selected electrical systems and appliances such as a small television set, kitchen clock, and even the front door's electronic latching device.

Doors and window frames are of a sandwich construction. The exterior and interior frames are held together with a special thermal-break material having an insulating, fire-retardant urethane foam core to prevent heat loss. It also guards against condensation on the interior surface frame.

The designers and builders of this house say that the efficiency possibilities in this unit are not dependent on the hot, sunny Tucson climate. The solar energy storage technology is at a sufficiently advanced state to make solar-assisted homes practical as far north as Canada.

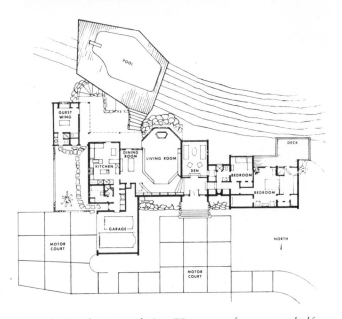

Decade 80 Solar House derives 75 percent of power needed for cooling and 100 percent of power for heating from the sun. Here are two views of the house plus a floor plan (The Copper Development Association).

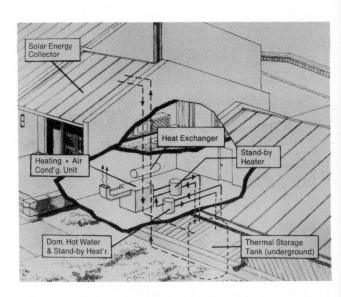

Schematic of solar collector system used to make the Decade 80 Solar House almost self-sufficient in energy. Thermal storage tank of 3,000-gallon capacity is used to power the home on cloudy days (The Copper Development Association).

DISCOVERY '76 SOLAR HOUSE

Discovery '76 Solar House is a project being undertaken at the University of Texas to test out various energy-saving systems. A three-bedroom house of contemporaary design, the unit has 1,950 square feet of living area.

The house was created with an enlarged mechanical room to accommodate a conventional mechanical system and a solar-energy storage system. Solar-energy collectors are installed on the roof. The heart of this house is, of course, the solar collector. This high efficiency, high temperature collector has a sophisticated tracking mechanism to obtain maximum concentration of solar energy. The solar system uses 42 collectors with a total of 420 square feet of collector surface.

The storage system consists of three 1,200 gallon tanks designated as high, medium and low temperature. The high and medium temperature tanks are identical, pressure-rated fiberglass tanks with a high temperature resin liner to protect the fiberglass from blistering. These tanks can stand temperatures up to 250 degrees. The third tank holds chilled water at 34 degrees.

The natural shading of glazed areas of the house, coupled with the use of insulated glass, holds down heat transfer. The doors used were constructed with insulation sandwiched between their surfaces. Both rigid urethane sheets and rock wool batts are used to insulate most of the walls and the roof. The house has about 50 percent more insulation than the typical single-family house.

This solar-assisted house was created by the University of Texas to evaluate various systems to achieve maximum energy saving. Floor plan and exterior of house show enlarged mechanical room next to garage breezeway (University of Texas at Arlington).

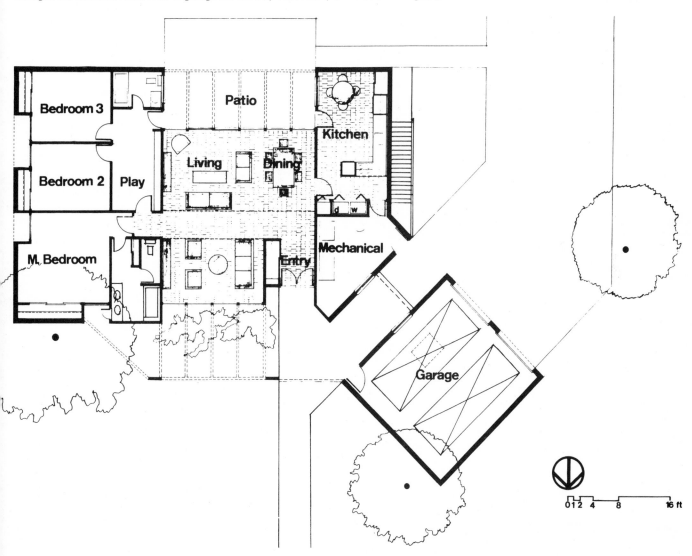

ANNUAL CYCLE ENERGY SYSTEM HOUSE

The Federal Energy Administration has designed what they feel is a house capable of cutting power bills by 50 percent. The unit, called The Annual Cycle Energy System (ACES) seeks to take advantage of the annual weather cycle in the U.S., which offers most people more heat than they need in the summer and more cold than they need in the winter.

The principal component of the ACES is an insulated tank of water which serves as an energy-storage bin. For well-insulated homes within the applicable zone (the geographic area between Atlanta, Georgia, and Minneapolis, Minnesota), this bin need not exceed two cubic feet of water for every square foot of living space.

Thus, a home with 1,500 square feet of living space would require a 3,000 cubic foot tank of water. This would be about the size of one-fourth to one-third of the basement. As a matter of fact, the energy bin could be located in the basement or could be built under the driveway, carport or patio of the house, depending on site conditions and design.

In this innovative system, heat is obtained from the bin during the winter by a heat pump which draws the heat from the water in much the same manner that the conventional home heat pump draws heat from the air. Heat drawn from the water is used to warm the building and to provide domestic hot water. This removal of heat from the water gradually turns the water into ice over a period of months.

In the summer months, the chilled water from the bin is used to provide air conditioning for the house without the operation of the heat pump compressor. This obviously causes the gradual melting of the ice over a period of months and thus stores heat for use in winter.

The purchase price of an ACES, says the Federal Energy Administration, depends on the size of the house. For most homes, however, it is estimated that the cost will be about $1,700 above the conventional central heating and cooling system. The cost of refitting an older home with such a system would be about $3,000.

The energy and money savings will also depend on the size of the residence and cost of electricity. It has been calculated that a residence containing 1,500 square feet will consume about 19,400 kilowatt hours per year in electric heating, air conditioning and water heating by conventional means. The same home equipped with an ACES system would consume only 7,400 kilowatt hours for the same functions. In an area where power cost is 3½¢ per kilowatt hour, the ACES system provides an operating cost saving of approximately $400 per year. Where the electrical cost is higher, the savings will be higher.

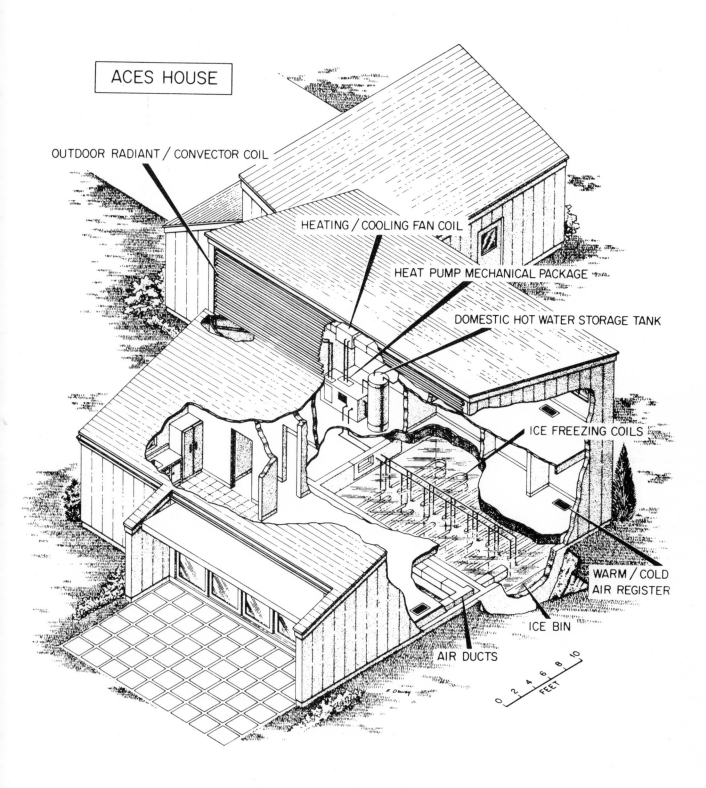

ACES HOUSE

OUTDOOR RADIANT / CONVECTOR COIL

HEATING / COOLING FAN COIL

HEAT PUMP MECHANICAL PACKAGE

DOMESTIC HOT WATER STORAGE TANK

ICE FREEZING COILS

WARM / COLD AIR REGISTER

ICE BIN

AIR DUCTS

0 2 4 6 8 10 FEET

Annual Cycle Energy System House (ACES) works on the principle of heat storage. In tanks located in basement or in driveway, a heat pump draws heat from the tank filled with water for winter heating. As the heat is used, the water gradually becomes ice. Then during the summer, this ice is used to keep house cool. In the process it heats up and again has heat stored for winter use (Federal Energy Administration).

OTHER ENERGY HOUSES UNDERWAY

There are a variety of energy houses going up all over the country. Many are under the sponsorship of local utilities, building materials manufacturers, and universities. Many individuals as well are undertaking projects. With each, the intent is the same: to lower energy bills by greater energy conservation or by use of radiant energy from the sun, thereby tapping a "free" source.

The Pacific Power & Light Co., Portland, Oregon, for example, is working closely with others on the construction of an energy conservation house called TERA One. The unit is a research model which incorporates large windows to trap sun on the south while much of the north wall is below grade to conserve energy.

The Southern California Gas Company is experimenting with two Minimum Energy Dwelling (MED) homes under a contract from the Federal Energy Administration. One house is occupied by a family and the other is a demonstration model. Special features incorporated in the homes include solar-assisted gas water-heating and comfort-heating and cooling systems, advanced and more efficient kitchen appliances, double-pane windows and thicker and better insulated walls and ceilings.

If you are interested in building a home which is highly energy efficient, check with your local utilities, universities, and home builder organizations to determine if any have been built in your area. Also, when hiring an architect have him incorporate many of the energy-saving features described in this chapter.

TERA One house is an experimental energy saving house built by the Pacific Power & Light Company in cooperation with others to trap sun on south side while north side is below grade.

MINIMUM ENERGY DWELLING
EXTERIOR

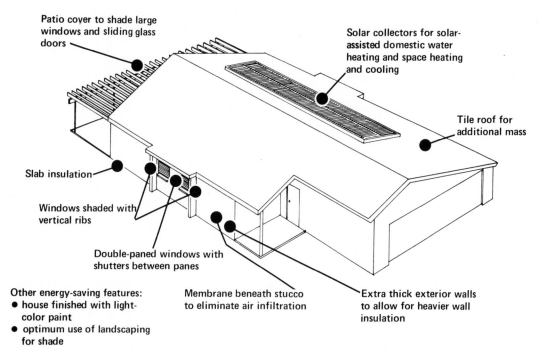

Patio cover to shade large windows and sliding glass doors

Solar collectors for solar-assisted domestic water heating and space heating and cooling

Tile roof for additional mass

Slab insulation

Windows shaded with vertical ribs

Double-paned windows with shutters between panes

Other energy-saving features:
- house finished with light-color paint
- optimum use of landscaping for shade

Membrane beneath stucco to eliminate air infiltration

Extra thick exterior walls to allow for heavier wall insulation

Minimum Energy Dwellings (MED) incorporate latest energy-saving features, including highly efficient kitchen appliances (Southern California Gas Company).

MINIMUM ENERGY DWELLING
INTERIOR

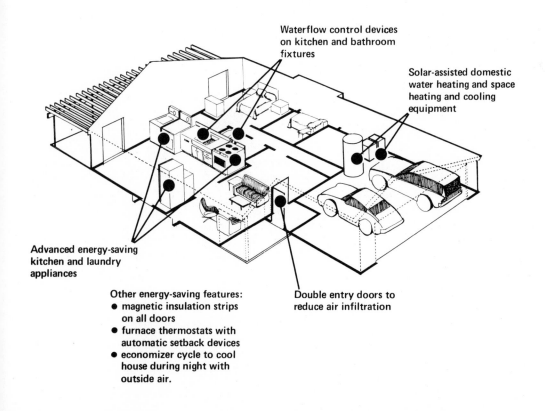

Waterflow control devices on kitchen and bathroom fixtures

Solar-assisted domestic water heating and space heating and cooling equipment

Advanced energy-saving kitchen and laundry appliances

Other energy-saving features:
- magnetic insulation strips on all doors
- furnace thermostats with automatic setback devices
- economizer cycle to cool house during night with outside air.

Double entry doors to reduce air infiltration

11. Seasonal House Check

Keeping your home in top shape so that it protects your family from harsh winters or sweltering summers is the key to comfort all year 'round. But in addition, home maintenance can cut your energy bills to the bone. The time to check your house is in the fall and spring. Don't skimp—by checking both seasons, you'll grab an economic advantage which is immeasurable for the season ahead. Spring and fall weather permit you to open and close doors and windows without losing any heated or cooled air. The check lists which follow can serve as a reminder for each season's bill-cutting maintenance program.

FALL CHECK LIST

1. Check insulation wherever possible—unfinished space such as basements or attics. Make sure it is thick enough and in good condition. Watch out for dampness. Replace or add necessary insulation (see Chapter 1 for your specific needs).

Here a homeowner is checking friction-fit insulation in his basement before the "heating season" comes around. Insulation which has "drooped" away from the basement ceiling is inspected for damage and replaced to fit snugly (Gary Smith).

2. Look closely at all weather stripping and caulking around your windows and doors. Look at joints and frames of doors and windows. Make sure caulking is not cracked or in disrepair. See if weather stripping fits firmly around the moving parts and is not worn out (see Chapter 2).

3. Check storm windows. Clean them and repair any cracks. Look at weather stripping and make any repairs necessary; make sure storms slide up and down as they should. Storm frames should also be checked for caulking problems. When you put on storms, take down screens and store them. This way you will get as much light as possible.

4. Put on your weatherproof air-conditioner cover if your air conditioner is left in the window or outside the house over the winter months. Make sure your cover fits properly and has no rips or tears.

5. Clean all your gutters and drain pipes. Usually it's best to wait until all falling leaves around your house have had their full season.

6. Service oil heating systems and heat pumps. If you have a forced air system, vacuum the ducts and grille-work. You should also change your filter and check pilot light on gas-fired systems. Have your serviceperson do annual maintenance.

7. Make sure your heating system is balanced (see Chapter 3) and correct it if it is not.

8. Drain hot water heater and remove sediment from bottom of tank. In some cases only a pail or two of water removed from the bottom of the tank is necessary to do the job.

9. If you have a gas- or oil-fired hot water heater, clean burner surfaces.

10. Have burners adjusted on hot water heaters to make them give even, efficient heat. Check electrodes, if your system has them, to be sure they are clean.

11. Check all your faucets and replace washers on your leaky ones.

12. Look at your outside faucets and drain them so that water won't freeze in the pipes. Then make sure that where the faucet pipe meets the frame of the house, the caulking around it is good and tight.

13. Check your roof for leaks. If you have an unfinished attic, you can check the inside for water stains, marks or actual holes. Make repairs to see if

the insulation was damaged by the weather. You may, if you have a finished attic interior, have to go up on the roof to check it. Replace or repair any damaged tiles or other roofing material.

14. Clean all lighting surfaces; take down all your fixtures wherever possible. More light and less wattage will thus be offered during winter.

15. Check for cracks and holes in the house siding. Fill with caulking.

16. Check and clean humidifier in accordance with your manufacturer's instruction manual.

17. Check chimney flue; clean obstructions, if any, and get it into good working order. Make sure your damper closes tightly!

18. Check hot water pipes if passing through uninsulated areas. See that the pipes are insulated.

19. Take down awnings used in summer and store carefully.

20 Clean refrigerator coils.

21. Change to winter schedule of off-peak hour use of electricity.

A good Fall inspection of your fireplace damper may include using a mirror as shown above. You will quickly be able to spot any outside light coming down the chimney around a loose fitting damper. If this is the case it should be corrected to fit tightly (Gary Smith).

SPRING CHECK LIST

1. Check winter damage to your house especially if you use an air conditioner. Look carefully around windows and doors for any possible air leak. Caulk or weather strip as necessary.

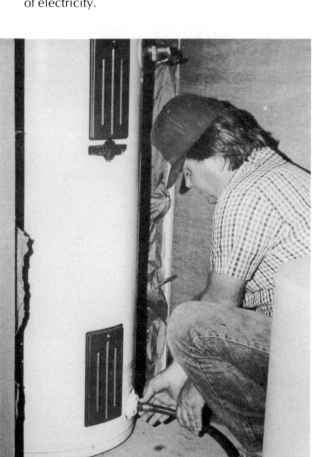

Draining your hot-water heater is done here by attaching a hose and letting the water run outside into the garden. This should remove the sediment that collects at the bottom of the tank (Gary Smith).

Spring and Fall, you should inspect your windows and doors for air leaks. Here, the weather stripping is being closely checked for winter damage (Gary Smith).

121

2. Go over attic very closely and note any moisture or ventilation problems. Clean the attic so that there is as little dust and dirt as possible. Make sure your attic vents are clean and bug-free. Clean power vents according to manufacturer's instructions.

3. Look at the outside of your house for cracks—peeling paint may be an indication of future problems. Paint, if you think that it's the time, in order to protect your house from the elements more efficiently.

4. Check drapes and blinds. Clean them and make sure they're in good working order to protect you from hot sunshine streaming in during the summer.

5. If you have awnings, take them out of storage, check them, and install for summer cooling aid.

6. Go over all your screens on windows and doors and look carefully for rips and tears. Patch or replace immediately.

7. Put up cleaned screens and take down storms. If you store your storms, do so carefully, noting which storm belongs to which window.

8. Check the filter on your air conditioner (take off winter cover if unit remained in windows over the winter) and service the air conditioner. Look and see if any leaves or grass have accumulated on or around the machine. If so, clean the area.

9. For gas or oil heat, have serviceperson switch off pilot light.

10. Check dryer vent and make sure it's working properly. If there isn't one, install vent as soon as possible.

11. Change to summer schedule of off-peak hour use of electricity.

12. Check stove hood and room fans. Clean and get into shape for summer use.

13. Have all your heat thermostats turned to the ''off'' position.

14. Check seals on refrigerators and freezers (see Chapter 6) and clean refrigerator coils.

15. Clean fireplace, and if your home is not air conditioned, keep the fireplace damper opened for better ventilation.

16. Plant shrubs, trees, etc. which you have found will act as shade savers or wind barriers.

17. Check basement for dampness. If too moist, remedy the situation with special paint or dehumidifier.

18. Get your dehumidifer into good working condition by cleaning according to manufacturer's instructions.

19. Check leaky faucets and replace washers wherever necessary.

12. Appendices

CHECKING FOR ENERGY EFFICIENCY IN THE OLDER HOME

Unless you find that rare buy, virtually any older dwelling you purchase will need considerable work to make it energy efficient. Although you cannot expect a totally efficient older house, there are some criteria to help you make a wise purchase.

When seriously considering the purchase of a particular house, ask the present owner for the past two or three years of energy receipts to gauge what it costs to heat, cool and light the unit. If the house is between 1,500 square feet and 2,000 square feet, under $600 a year for lighting and heating is quite good. Between $600 and $800 is acceptable. If the annual bill ranges between $800 and $1000, it is fair. A bill between $1000 and $1200 is poor. If over $1200 a year, you should consider asking the seller for a reduced price so you can apply the savings to energy-conservation features to make the house livable at a reasonable cost.

Checking for Efficiency

The following checks will furnish you with a rough idea of how energy-tight the house is. For a complete check, hire a home inspection service, which will furnish you with a good evaluation of the unit—before you purchase. Such a service costs between $75 and $150.

Insulation. Ideally, every house should have *all* walls, ceilings, and floors that face the exterior insulated. Begin with the attic and work down. The attic should have insulation *either* in the attic floor *or* between roof rafters and end walls. All dormers and spaces around windows should have insulation stuffed into cracks.

All side walls facing the exterior should be insulated. Floors over unheated garages or basements should have insulation in the floor. This applies to houses built over crawl spaces as well. Houses with enclosed crawl spaces may not have insulation in the floor. If not, then insulation should be in crawl space walls. For more complete details on insulation, see Chapter 1.

Windows. All houses with single-pane glass need well weather stripped storm windows to be energy efficient. If the house you are thinking about buying is relatively old, then it won't have modern double-glazed glass in it. If the house does not have storm windows, this will be a considerable outlay of cash for you. Perhaps you can ask the seller to reduce price or furnish storms. In most older houses, windows will probably have to be caulked to reduce air infiltration.

Doors. Storm doors should be included for energy efficiency. If doors are in poor shape, they should be replaced with energy-efficient insulated doors. If standing by an exterior door you can see the light of day when the door is closed, weather stripping is in poor shape and will have to be replaced.

Heating and cooling system. The most cost-saving system currently available is a gas-fired heating system with electric air conditioning. If the choice of two homes comes down to the heating system, take the one with gas. Oil and heat pumps should be a second choice. An all-electric home should be your last choice, if the climate is at all cold.

Ventilation. The attic can be checked for adequate ventilation. Either with static vents or power vents, the attic should be dry and relatively cool. If you are looking at a house in the summer and the attic is hot, there is not enough ventilation. If it is winter and the attic is damp, this is another sign that ventilation is lacking. If there seems to be considerable moisture buildup in the attic, bring in a home-inspection service to determine whether or not there is structural damage in this space. A rotten attic could cost you many thousands of dollars to repair. *

Lighting. Lighting costs vary with the user and this is a cost you can control. If the house contains many flourescent fixtures, task-lighting and other energy conservors, there are that many less you will have to replace. Keep an eye out for bullet lamps. These lamps are recessed into the ceiling and usually penetrate the insulation, causing an energy leak.

Alternate heating sources. If the house has a fireplace, it *must* have a damper installed and closed (when the unit is not in use) or it will begin costing you money right away. If a very old masonry fireplace is in the house, it might be wise to get an estimate from a local contractor on how much a new damper will cost before you purchase the home.

These are only a few things to look for when buying a home. Previous chapters dealing with each of the above subjects will furnish you with additional, more in-depth knowledge.

*Or, for more specifics, consult *Finding & Fixing the Older Home*, a *Successful* book by Joseph Schram.

GLOSSARY

Air changes—replacement of air in a room over a period of time. When air is replaced several times an hour it is referred to as air changes per hour.

Ambient temperature—refers to the temperature out of doors.

Awning window—a projecting window, hinged at the top, opening up and out like an awning.

Air infiltration—outdoor air leaking into a structure uncontrollably. Due mainly to cracks in the structure, around door and window frames. Air infiltration will increase greatly as the air pressure, due to increased wind velocity, increases. In a well-built house, the air infiltration may be less than ¼ air change per hour. In a poorly built home, air infiltration could be as high as 2 or more air changes an hour.

Bay window—composed of 3 or more individual windows generally with the side or flanker units at 45 degree or 30 degree angles to the wall. A bay projects from the wall of the structure.

Boiler—a unit which heats water or produces steam. It includes a burner, heat exchanger, flue and container.

Bow window—3 or more individual windows in a gently curved contour. Bow windows project from the wall of the structure.

British thermal unit (Btu)—unit of thermal energy equal to the amount of heat required to raise the temperature of one pound of water one degree Fahrenheit at or near 39.2 degrees Fahrenheit, its temperature of maximum density. Example: to increase the temperature of 4 pounds of water 100 degrees would require 400 Btu. Generally speaking, one Btu is about equal to the amount of heat given off by a common wooden match.

British thermal units per hour—usually abbreviated Btuh, this term refers to heat generation. Heating and cooling systems are usually rated in Btuh. That is, if a boiler is capable of producing 50,000 Btu's of heat in an hour its rating is 50,000 Btuh.

Casement window—a projecting window hinged at the sides, usually opening outward like a door.

C.F.M.—an abreviation for cubic feet per minute. This term usually refers to cubic feet per minute (cfm) of air change.

Caulking—a flexible material used to seal up cracks or spaces in a structure.

Comfort region—range of temperatures and humidity of room air in which approximately 50 percent of adults feel comfortable.

Condensation—droplets of water and sometimes frost (in extremely cold climates) which accumulate on the inside of the exterior covering of a building.

Conduction—method of heat transfer where heat moves through a solid.

Conduit, electrical—a pipe, usually metal, in which wire is installed.

Convection—method of heat transfer where heat moves by motion of a fluid or gas, usually air.

Degree days—degree days or (DD) is the average of the daily maximum and minimum temperatures for any given day. The degree day value for any given day is the difference between 65 degrees and the mean daily temperature. For instance, if the mean daily temperature is 50 degrees, the degree days are 65 minus 50 or 15 degree days. As the temperature goes lower, the degree days increase. If the temperature is above 65 degrees, they are not counted. This is a very useful term in establishing fuel needs and potential energy-conservation needs for a particular geographic region.

Degree Fahrenheit—the temperature scale generally accepted in the United States. On this scale, water freezes at 32 degrees and boils at 212 degrees.

Design temperature difference—the difference in temperature between the indoor temperature and the outdoor temperature for a given locality. In most sections of the U.S. there is a design temperature difference of 75 degrees but in more northerly climates it can be 95 degrees.

Dormer—a projection on a sloping roof, the vertical wall framing for windows.

Double-hung window—two vertically sliding sash which bypass each other in a single frame. Sash may be counter-balanced by weights or springs.

Eaves—a roof overhang which projects over the walls.

Energy efficiency ratio—the cooling energy output of an air conditioner divided by the kilowatt input.

Flashing—a metal or plastic strip attached to the outside of window jambs to provide a weather barrier preventing leakage between the frame and the wall.

Flue—the space in a chimney through which fumes (smoke, gases) travel to the outdoors.

Frame—outside portion of a window unit which encloses the sash. Composed of side jambs, head jamb and sill.

Frostline—the depth to which frost penetrates into the soil. This line varies from one part of the country to another and varies in one locality from one winter to another. Footings must always be placed below the frostline.

Furnace—a unit, similar to a boiler, used to heat air.

Gable end louvers—a fixed attic vent. Gable end louvers are the triangular shaped louvers mounted in the top point of the gable. Because they are inexpensive and somewhat inconspicuous they have been a popular type of attic vent and are manufactured in a wide range of sizes.

Glass, insulating—two sheets of glass bonded together in a unit to enclose a captive air space.

Glazing, single—a single sheet of glass installed in a window sash.

Glazing, double—a single glazed sash with an additional glass panel installed on the sash to provide an air space between the two lights of glass. The second glass can either be movable or fixed and can be installed on either the inside or outside of the sash. Double glazing differs from insulating glass in that there is no positive seal around the edges of the two panes of glass to provide a true dead air space.

Glazing, triple—a sash glazed with 3 panes of glass, enclosing 2 separate air spaces. This can be accomplished by applying a storm panel to a sash that is glazed with insulating glass, or on some units by applying inside and outside storm panels to a single glazed sash.

Heat conductor—any material which allows heat to pass through it quickly. Glass and metal are typical examples of good heat conductors.

Heat pump—a combination heating and cooling device. In the winter it extracts heat from the air as cold as 20 degrees, and in the summer it works in reverse to become an air conditioner.

Heat transfer, conduction—heat transfer through a solid. A typical example is when a metal spoon is placed in a hot cup of liquid. The portion of the metal spoon not submerged quickly heats up by conduction. In homes, a typical example of heat loss by conduction is through window panes. To slow this heat transfer, use double-pane glass.

Heat transfer, convection—the transfer of heat from one object to another by the movement of air, water or another fluid.

Heat transfer, radiation—whenever one object is warmer than another, heat energy will be transmitted across space by radiation. The sun radiates light to the earth which is transferred into heat. If you stand in front of a fireplace, the air around you may be cool but your body will be warmed by the burning logs through radiation.

Horizontal sliding windows—the sash in this type of window slides horizontally. Usually there are two movable sashes but often one is fixed.

In-door design temperature—heating experts select an in-door air temperature when determining the heat loss of a structure. This term is useful in selecting the capacity of heating equipment for a room or structure. Earlier in this century the standard in-door design temperature was 70 degrees, today it is 75 degrees.

Insulation—any one of a number of materials used to lower the transfer of heat from inside a structure to outside. In single-family homes, typical placement of insulation includes all exterior walls, roof or top floor ceiling, in basement or crawl space.

Insulating value or "R" value—all insulation materials commercially available have an "R" value printed on the package. This "R" value is the resistance to heat transfer that the material possesses. Every material has at least some "R" value but many, such as glass, are quite low. Mineral wool, and other types of insulation, have an "R" value of about 3 per inch. Therefore, if you wanted a wall with an "R-12" rating, you would have to install about 3¾ inches of insulation. The entire 4 inches of insulation is not necessary because siding and interior finishes have at least some "R" value.

Insulators—all materials conduct heat to one degree or another, but materials which conduct heat slowly are called heat insulators. Materials commonly used as insulators include particleboard, perlite or vermiculite, cellulose fibers, mineral wool and others.

Kilowatt hour—this is a unit of electrical consumption and is said to equal about 3,400 Btu's.

Picture window—a large stationary (nonventilating) window which is designed for a maximum view without obstruction.

Plenum—found in forced hot air heating systems, a large duct used as a distributor for the hot air from the furnace going to different parts of the house via smaller ducts leaving the plenum.

Rectangular louvers—a fixed attic vent. These units are sometimes mounted in the gable ends of the attic to serve as ventilation intake and exhaust, similar to gable end louvers.

Reflectance—a property of a material indicating the percentage of light that is reflected when a certain amount of light strikes the surface. The amount of light not reflected is either absorbed, or passes through the material. A porous black surface will absorb considerably more light than a light surface. When light falls on a standard pane of glass, most passes through, although some light is reflected.

Relative humidity—this is a measurement, expressed as a percentage, indicating the amount of water vapor in the air compared to the amount that the air could contain if it were completely saturated with moisture.

Roof louvers—fixed attic vent. Roof louvers are small domes mounted near the ridge of the roof. Some have a type of baffle designed to improve air flow and reduce weather infiltration. Others have a turbine wheel actuated by the wind and intended to draw air out of the attic.

Sash—the framework holding the glass in a window unit. Composed of stiles (sides) and rails (top and bottom).

Shims—Wood wedges (often wood shingles) used to secure the window or door unit in the rough or masonry opening in a square, level and plumb position during and after installation.

Sliding window—a window with two or more sash that slide past each other within the frame. They may slide horizontally or vertically as in a double-hung window.

Storm sash or storm window—the extra layer of window usually but not always placed on the outside of an existing window. This affords additional protection against air infiltration and heat loss by conduction.

Thermal barrier—a strip of nonconducting material, such as wood, vinyl or foam rubber, separating the inside and outside surfaces of a metal window sash or frame, or a metal door or sill, to stop the conduction of heat to the outside and the resulting cold surfaces inside.

Vapor barrier—material used to slow or stop the movement of water vapor into walls or spaces such as attics. When adding insulation to walls, the vapor barrier must always be placed on the warm side of the wall to prevent penetration of the water vapor into the wall.

Vent—anything that allows air to flow in and out of a space. While vents can become very sophisticated, open windows and doors can act as vents.

Ventilation—the introduction of air into a space, such as a house, by some controlled mechanical system or unit. Ventilation is controlled by louvers, fans and opening windows, among other methods.

Weather stripping—metal, plastic or felt strips designed to seal between windows and door frames to prevent air infiltration.

MANUFACTURERS

Air Conditioning

Airtemp Div., Chrysler Corp.
1600 Webster St.
Dayton, OH 45404

Arkla Air Conditioning
Arkla Ind. Inc.
400 E. Capital
Little Rock, AR 72203

Bryant Air Conditioning Co.
7310 W. Morris St.
Indianapolis, IN 46231

Carrier Air Conditioning Co.
Carrier Parkway
Syracuse, NY 13201

Day & Night Co.
855 Anaheim-Puente Rd.
La Puente, CA 91749

Fasco Ind. Inc.
P.O. Box 150
Fayetteville, NC 28302

Heil-Quaker Corp.
647 Thomason Lane
Nashville, TN 37204

Hotpoint
Appliance Park
Louisville, KY 40225

Janitrol Div., Andro Corp.
400 Dublin Ave.
Columbus, OH 43215

Johnson Corp.
421 Monroe St.
Bellevue, OH 44811

McGraw-Edison
704 Clark
Albion, MI 49224

Singer Co. Climate Control
Finderne Ave.
Somerville, NJ 08876

Trane Co.
3600 Pamel Creek Rd.
La Crosse, WI 54601

Westinghouse Electric Corp.
Major Appliance Sales
One Allegheny Square
Pittsburgh, PA 15212

Dishwashers

Admiral Corp.
3800 Cortland
Chicago, IL 60647

Caloric Corp.
Topton, PA 19562

Chambers Corp.
Taylor Rd.
Oxford, MS 38655

General Electric Co.
Appliance Park
Louisville, KY 40225

Gibson Appliance Corp.
Greenville, MI 48838

Hotpoint
Appliance Park
Louisville, KY 40225

KitchenAid
The Hobart Mfg. Co.
Troy, OH 45374

Magic Chef Inc.
P.O. Box 717
Cleveland, TN 37311

Modern Maid Inc.
E. 14 St.
Chattanooga, TN 37301

Roper Sales
1905 W. Court
Kankakee, IL 60901

Speed Queen
A McGraw- Edison Co.
Commercial Sales
Shepard St.
Ripon, WI 54971

Westinghouse Electric Corp.
Major Appliance Sales
One Allegheny Square
Pittsburgh, PA 15212

Whirlpool Corp.
Benton Harbor, MI 49022

Fireplaces and Equipment

Cadet Mfg. Co.
2500 W. Fouth Plain Blvd.
Vancouver, WA 98663

Dura-Vent
2525 El Camino Real
Redwood City, CA 94064

Dyna Mfg. Co. Inc.
2540 Industry Way
Lynwood, CA 90262

Fasco Ind. Inc.
P.O. Box 150
Fayetteville, NC 28302

Heatilator Fireplace
Div. Vega Ind. Inc.
P.O. Box 409
Mt. Pleasant, IA 52641

Leigh Products Inc.
Coppersville, MI 49404

The Majestic Co.
245 Erie St.
Huntington, IN 46750

Malm Metal Products Inc.
2640 Santa Rosa Ave.
Santa Rosa, CA 95401

Martin Inc.
3414 Governors Drive
Huntsville, AL 35801

Preway Inc.
1430 Second St.
Wisconsin Rapids, WI 54494

Superior Fireplace Co.
P.O. Box 2066
4325 Artesia Ave.
Fullerton, CA 92633

U.S. Stove Co.
S. Pittsburgh, TN 37380

Vega Industries
P.O. Box 409
Mt. Pleasant, IA 52641

Washington Stove Works
P.O. Box 687
Everett, WA 98201

Glass & Glazing

ASG Industries Inc.
P.O. Box 929
Kingsport, TN 37662

DAP Inc.
P.O. Box 277
Dayton, OH 45401

Dearborn Glass Co.
6600 S. Harlem Ave.
Bedford Park, IL 60638

Libbey-Owens-Ford Co.
811 Madison Ave.
Toledo, OH 43695

PPG Industries
One Gateway Center
Pittsburgh, PA 15222

Pittsburgh Corning Corp.
Three Gateway Center
Pittsburgh, PA 15222

Season All Industries
Indiana, PA 15701

Heating Systems

Addison Products Co.
P.O. Box 100
Addison, MI 49220

Ammark Corp.
12-22 River Rd.
Fairlawn, NJ 07410

Arkla Air Conditioning
Div. Arkla Ind. Inc.
400 E. Capital
Little Rock, AR 72203

Bryant Air Conditioning Co.
7310 W. Morris St.
Indianapolis, IN 46231

Cadet Mfg. Co.
2500 W. Fourth Plain Blvd.
P.O. Box 1685
Vancouver, WA 98663

Crane Co.
300 Park Ave.
New York, NY 10022

Day & Night Co.
855 Anaheim-Puente Rd.
La Puente, CA 91749

Emerson Electric Co.
Chromalox Comfort Condition Div.
8100 W. Florissant Ave.
St. Louis, MO 63136

Fasco Industries Inc.
P.O. Box 150
Fayetteville, NC 28302

Federal Pacific Electric Co.
150 Ave. L
Newark, NJ 07101

General Electric Co.
Appliance Park
Louisville, KY 40225

Heat Controller Inc.
1900 Wellworth Ave.
Jackson, MI 49203

Heil-Quaker Corp.
647 Thomason Lane
Nashville, TN 37204

Johnson Corp.
421 Monroe St.
Bellevue, OH 44811

Kewanee Boiler
101 Franklin St.
Kewanee, IL

Trane Co.
3600 Pammel Creek Rd.
La Crosse, WI 54601

Humidifiers & Dehumidifiers

Bryant Air Conditioning Co.
7310 W. Morris St.
Indianapolis, IN 46231

Dayton Electric Mfg. Co.
5959 W. Howard St.
Chicago, IL 60648

General Electric Co.
Appliance Park
Louisville, KY 40225

Heat Controller Inc.
1900 Wellworth Ave.
Jackson, MI 49203

Hermidifier Co. Inc.
P.O. Box 1747
Lancaster, PA 17604

Home Siegler Div.
Lear Siegler Inc.
15929 East Valley Blvd.
Industry, CA 91744

Leigh Products Inc.
Coopersville, MI 49404

Porter H.K. Co.
Porter Bldg.
Pittsburgh, PA 15219

Trane Co.
3600 Pammel Creek Rd.
La Crosse, WI 54601

Insulation

Celotex Corp.
1500 N. Dale Mabry
Tampa, FL 33607

Certain-Teed Products Corp.
Shelter Materials Group
P.O. Box 860
Valley Forge, PA 19482

DeVac, Inc.
10130 Highway 55
Minneapolis, MN 55441

E.I. Dupont,
Prod. Info. Section
1007 Market Street
Wilmington, DE 19898

Flintkote Co.
480 Central Ave.
E. Rutherford Ave., NJ 07073

General Aluminum Western Div.
4850 Irving Street
Boise, ID 83704

Globe Industries Inc.
2638 E. 126 St.
Chicago, IL 60636

Gold Bond Building Prod. Div.
National Gypsum Co.
325 Delaware Ave.
Buffalo, NY 14202

Grace, W.r. & Co.,
Construction Prod. Div.
62 Whittemore Ave.
Cambridge, MA 02140

Homasote Co.
P.O. Box 240
W. Trenton, NJ 08628

Johns-Manville
Denver, CO 80217

National Cellulose Corp.
12315 Robin Blvd.
Houston, TX

National Gypsum Co.
325 Delaware Ave.
Buffalo, NY 12832

Norton Co.
Sealant Operations
Granville, NY 14202

Owens-Corning Fiberglas Corp.
Fiberglas Tower
Toledo, OH 43601

PPG Industries
One Gateway Center
Pittsburgh, PA 15222

Porter H.K. Company
Porter Bldg.
Pittsburgh, PA 15222

Season All Industries, Inc.
Indiana, PA 15701

Temple Ind.
Diboll, TX 74941

Therma-Coustics, Inc.
21900 Main St.
P.O. Box 190
Colton, CA 92324

Thermtron Prod. Inc.
P.O. Box 9146 Baer Filed
Fort Wayne, IN 46809

U.S. Mineral Prods. Co.
Stanhope, NJ 07874

U.S. Plywood Div.
Champion-International
1 Landmark Sq.
Stamford, CT

Weyerhaeuser Co.
Tacoma, WA 98401

Laundry Equipment & Accessories

Admiral Corp.
3800 Cortland
Chicago, IL 60647

All Products, Inc.
251 E. Fifth St.
St. Paul, MN 55101

Fednor Corp.
Woodbridge Ave.
Edison, NJ 08817

General Electric Co.
Appliance Park
Louisville, KY 40225

Gibson Appliance Corp.
Greenville, MI 48838

Goodwin of California, Inc.
1075 Second St.
Berkeley, CA 94710

Guy Gray Mfg. Co. Inc.
P.O. Box 771 Blandville Rd.
Paducah, KY 42001

Hide-A-Dri Div.
Russell Aluminum Corp.
5700 N.V. 37 Ave.
Miami, FL

Hotpoint
Appliance Park
Louisville, KY 40225

Martin Reel Co.
30 E. Main St.
Mohawk, NY 10549

Maytag Co.
Newton, IA 50208

Modern Maid, Inc.
E. 14 St.
Chattanooga, TN 37301

Mustee & Sons, Inc.
6911 Lorain Ave.
Cleveland, OH 44102

Service Distributors Inc.
567 Seventh St.
San Francisco, CA 94103

Speed Queen
A McGraw-Edison Co.
Commercial Sales
Shepard St.
Ripon, WI. 54971

Symmons Industries, Inc.
31 Brooks Dr.
Braintree, MA 02184

Union Brass & Metal Mfg.
501 W. Lawson Ave.
St. Paul, MN 55117

Wascomat of America
461 Doughty Blvd.
Inwood, NY 11696

Lighting

Art Metal Lighting
ITT Lighting Fixture Div.
P.O. Box 195
Vermillion, OH 44103

Artolier Div.
Emerson Electric Co.
141 Lanza Ave.
Garfield, NJ 07026

B&L Lighting Co.
579 N. Mountain Rd.
Newington, CT 04111

Bell Electric Co.
2600 W. 50th St.
Chicago, IL 60632

Bryant Electric
Div. of Westinghouse
1421 State St.
Bridgeport, CT 06602

Century Lamp Co.
2463 E. 12 St.
Los Angeles, CA 90021

Champion Lighting Co., Inc.
152 W. 25th St.
Hialeah, FL 33010

Corbett Lighting, Inc.
2955 Anode Lane
Dallas, TX 75220

Diamond Lighting Fixture Corp.
307 Richardson St.
Brooklyn, NY 11222

Duro Test Corp.
2321 Kennedy Blvd.
North Bergen, NJ

General Lamp Co.
54 Bayview Ave.
Inwood, NY 11696

Globe Lighting Prod., Inc.
Valmont Industrial Park
Hazelton, PA 18201

Halo Lighting Div.
McGraw-Edison Co.
400 Busse Rd.
Elk Grove Village, IL 60007

International Lighting Mfg. Co.
1825 N. 19th St.
St. Louis, MO 63106

Kosman Lighting Equipment Co.
2201 3rd St.
San Francisco, CA 94107

The F H Lawson Co.
801 Evans St.
Cincinnati, OH 45204

Lightolier, Inc.
346 Claremont Ave.
Jersey City, NJ 07305

Luxo Lamp Co.
Monument Park
Port Chester, NY 10573

NuTone Div.
Scoville Mfg. Co.
Madison & Red Bank Rds.
Cincinnati, OH 45227

Superior Electric Co.
383 Middle St.
Bristol, CT 06010

Solar Lighting Corp.
1100 Washington Blvd.
Chicago, IL 60611

Swivilier Co., Inc.
33 Route 304
Nanuet, NY 10954

Virden Lighting
Div. of The Scott Fetzer Co.
6103 Longfellow Ave.
Cleveland, OH 44103

J.A. Wilson Lighting Co.
2001 Peninsula Dr.
Erie, PA 16512

Ranges / Ovens

Admiral Corp.
3800 Cortland
Chicago, IL 60647

Athens Stove Works Inc.
P.O. Box 10
Athens, TN 37303

Atlanta Stove Works
P.O. Box 5454
Atlanta, GA 30307

Autocrat Corp.
Illinois & Benton Sts.
New Athens, IL 62264

Brown Stove Works, Inc.
P.O. Box 490
Cleveland, TN 37311

Caloric Corp.
Topton, PA 19562

Chambers Corp.
Old Tayleo Rd.
Oxford, MS 38655

Corning Glass Works
Major Appliance Div.
Corning, NY 14830

Crown Stove Works
4627-35 W. 12th Place
Cicero, IL 60650

Distinctive Appliances
7251 Hinds Ave.
N. Hollywood, CA 91605

Eagle Range & Mfg. Co.
P.O. Box 489
Belleville, IL 62222

Empire Stove Co.
918 Freeburg Ave.
Belleville, IL 62222

General Electric Co.
Appliance Park
Louisville, KY 40225

Gerco, Inc.
3455 N.W. 54 St.
Miami, FL 33142

Gibson Appliance Corp.
Greenville, MI 48838

Hardwick Stove Co.
240 Edwards S.E.
Cleveland, TN 37311

Hotpoint, General Electric Co.
Appliance Park
Louisville, KY 40225

Jenn-Air Corp.
3035 Shadeland Ave.
Indianapolis, IN 46226

Keller Ind. Inc.
18000 St. Rd. 9
Miami, FL 33162

Magee Range Div.
Boston Stove Co.
Reading, MA

Magic Chef Inc.
P.O. Box 717
Cleveland, TN 37311

Modern Maid, Inc.
E. 14 St.
Chattenooga, TN 37301

Monarch Range Co.
Beaver Dam, WI 53916

Morgan-Wightman Supply Co.
Main P.O. Box 1
St. Louis, MO 63166

O'Keefe & Merritt Co.
3700 E. Olympic Blvd.
Los Angeles, CA 90023

The Pease Co.
900 Forest Ave.
Hamilton, OH 45013

Ronson Corp.
1 Ronson Rd.
Woodbridge, NJ 07095

Roper Sales
1905 W. Court
Kankakee, IL 60901

Speed Queen
A McGraw-Edison Co.
Commercial Sales
Shepard St.
Ripon, WI 54971

State Stove & Mfg. Co.
Ashland City, TN 37015

Sunray Stove Co.
Div. of Glenwood Range Co.
435 Park Ave.
Delaware, OH 43015

Thermador
Div. of Norris Industries
5119 District Blvd.
Los Angeles, CA 90022

Welbilt Corp.
57-18 Flushing Ave.
Maspeth, NY 11378

Westinghouse Electric Corp.
Major Appliance Sales
One Allegheny Square
Pittsburgh, PA 15212

Refrigerators / Freezers

Acme National Refrigeration Co.
19-26 Hazen St.
Astoria, NY 11105

Admiral Corp.
3800 Cortland
Chicago, IL 60647

Amana Refrigeration, Inc.
Amana, IA 52203

Dwyer Products Corp.
Calumet Ave.
Michigan City, IN 46360

Frigidaire Div.
General Motors Corp.
300 Taylor St.
Dayton, OH 45401

General Electric Co.
Appliance Park
Louisville, KY 40225

Gibson Appliance Corp.
Greenville, MI 48838

Hot Point Appliance
Appliance Park
Louisville, KY 40225

Kelvinator App. Co.
1545 Clyde Park Ave.
Grand Rapids, MI 49509

King Refrigerator Corp.
7602 Woodhaven Blvd.
Glendale, NY 11227

Magic Chef Inc.
P.O. Box 717
Cleveland, TN 37311

Norcold
1501 Michigan
Sidney, OH 45365

Phillips-Buttorff Corp.
P.O. Box 1129
Nashville, TN

Westinghouse Electric Corp.
Major Appliance Sales
One Allegheny Square
Pittsburgh, PA 15212

Skylights

Bell Skylights Div.
The Richard Grant Co.
2039 Pech Rd.
P.O. Box 55583
Houston, TX 77055

Cadillac Plastic & Chemical
15841 2 Ave.
Detroit, MI 48232

Dimensional Plastics Corp.
1065 E. 26 St.
Box 3337
Hialeah, FL 33013

Kosman Lighting Equipment Co.
2201 3rd St.
San Francisco, CA 94107

George C. Vaughan & Sons
223 S. Frio St.
San Antonio, TX 78207

Morgan-Wightman Supply Co.
Main P.O. Box 1
St. Louis, MO 63166

Solar Collectors & Devices

Arkla Ind. Inc.
950 E. Virginia St.
Evansville, IN 47701

Beutel Solar Heater Co.
1527 N. Miami Ave.
Miami, FL 33132

Edward's Engineering Corp.
101 Alexander Ave.
Pompton Plains, NJ 07444

Enthone, Inc.
Box 1900
New Haven, CT 06508

FAFCO
2860 Spring St.
Redwood City, CA 94063

Kalwall Corp.
P.O. Box 237
Manchester, NH 03105

Ram Products Co.
1111 N. Centerville Rd.
Sturgis, MI 49091

Solar Energy Co.
810 18 St., N.W.
Washington, D.C. 2006

Sunworks, Inc.
669 Boston Post Rd.
Guilford, CT 06437

Transparent Products Corp.
1727 W. Pico Blvd.
Los Angeles, CA 90015

Tranter Manufacturing Inc.
735 E. Hazel St.
Lansing, MI 48909

Ventilating Equipment

American Metal Products, Inc.
6100 Bandini Blvd.
Los Angeles, CA 90040

Aubrey Mfg. Co.
Union, IL 60180

Broan Mfg. Co. Inc.
P.O. Box 140
Hartford, WI 53027

Butler Engineering Co.
P.O. Box 728
Mineral Wells, TX 76067

Distinctive Appliances
7251 Hinds Ave.
N. Hollywood, CA 91605

Fasco Industries, Inc.
P.O. Box 150
Fayetteville, NC 28302

General Electric Co.
Appliance Park
Louisville, KY 40225

Glenwood Range Co.
140 Industrial Park
Taunton, MA 02780

Goodwin of California, Inc.
1075 Second St.
Berkeley, CA 94710

Gray & Dudley Co.
2300 Clifton Rd.
Nashville, TN 37209

H.C. Products Co.
Box 68
Princeville, IL 61159

ILG Industries, Inc.
2850 N. Pulaski Rd.
Chicago, IL 60641

Jensen Ind.
1946 East 46
Los Angeles, CA 90058

Kich-N-Vent Div.,
Home Metal Prod. Co.
750 Central Expressway
Plano, TX 75074

Kool-O-Matic Corp.
1831 Terminal Rd.
Niles, MI 49120

Leslie Locke Bldg. Prod. Co.
Ohio St.
Lodi, OH 44254

Louver Mfg. Co. Inc.
P.O. Box 519
2101 W. Main St.
Jacksonville, AR 72076

Modern Maid, Inc.
E. 14 St.
Chattanooga, TN 37301

Morgan-Wightman Supply Co.
Main P.O. Box 1
St. Louis, MO 63166

National Industries Inc.
1410 S.W. 12th Ave.
P.O. Box 293
Ocala, FL 32670

NuTone Div., Scovill Mfg. Co.
Madison & Red Bank Rds.
Cincinnati, OH 45227

Penn Ventilator Co. Inc.
11th St. & Allegheny Ave.
Philadelphia, PA 19140

Power Vent
185 E. South St.
Freeland, PA 18224

Rangaire Corp.
P.O. Box 177
Cleburne, TX 76031

Roper Sales
1905 W. Court
Kankakee, IL 60901

Sunray Stove Co.
Div. of Glenwood Range Co.
435 Park Ave.
Delaware, OH 43015

Thermador
Div. of Norris Industries
5119 District Blvd.
Los Angeles, CA 90022

Vent-A-Hood Co.
P.O. Box 426
Richardson, TX 75080

Water Heaters

Bryan System
Bryan Steam Corp.
P.O. Box 27
Peru, IN 46970

Dayton Elec. Mfg. Co.
5959 W. Howard St.
Chicago, IL 606048

Hydrotherm Inc.
Rockland Ave.
Northvale, NJ 07647

Megatherm Corp.
803 Taunton Ave.
E. Providence, RI 02914

Patterson-Kelley Co., Inc.
100 Burson St.
E. Stroudsburg, PA 18301

Precision Parts Corp.
400 No. 1st St.
Nashville, TN 37207

Rheem Mfg. Co.
Water Heating Products Div.
7600 South Kedzie Ave.
Chicago, IL 60652

A.O. Smith Corp.
Consumer Products Div.
Box 28
Kankakee, IL 60901

The Whalen Co.
Brock Bridge Rd.
Laurel, MD 20810

Wind Power Equipment

Aeromotor Div. of Brader Ind.
800 E. Dallas St.
Broken Arrow, OK 74012

Automatic Power, Inc.
Pennwalt Corp.
205 Hutcheson St.
Houston, TX 77003

Bucknell Engineering Co.
10717 E. Rush St.
El Monte, CA 91733

Dyna Technology Inc.
P.O. Box 3263
Sioux City, IA 51102

O'Brock Windmill Sales
Rte. 1, 12 St.
North Benton, OH 44449

Windows

ALCOA
1501 Alcoa Bldg.
Pittsburgh, PA 15219

Allastics Div.,
Sub. of Bethlehem Steel
1275 Enterprise Drive
Narcross, GA 30071

Alsar, Inc.
21121 Telegraph Rd.
Southfield, MI 48075

American Alum Window Corp.
767 Eastern Ave.
Malden, MA 02148

Anderson Corp.
Bayport, MN 55003

Burton Wood Work
Burton Enterprises Inc.
Mac Arthur Ave.
Cobleskill, NY 12043

Capitol Prod. Corp.
P.O. Box 69
Mechanicsburg, PA 17055

Caradoo Window & Door Div.
Scovill Mfg. Co.
1098 Jackson St.
Dubuque, IA 52001

Carmel Steel Prods.
13821 Marquardt Ave.
Sante Fe Springs, CA 90670

Certain-Teed Products Corp.
Ideal Co. Div.
Box 889
Waco, TX 76703

Crossly Window
7375 N.W. 35th Ave.
Miami, FL 33147

DeVac, Inc.
10130 Highway 55
Minneapolis, MN 55441

General Aluminum Western Div.
4850 Irving St.
Boise, ID 83704

International Window Corp.
5626 E. Firestone Blvd.
S. Gate, CA 90280

Kawneer Co.
1105 N. Front St.
Biles, MI 49120

Keller Ind. Inc.
18000 St. Rd. 9
Miami, FL 33162

Louisiana-Pacific Corp.
Weather-Seal Div.
324 Wooster Rd. North
Barbeton, OH 44203

Malta, A Division of Philips Industries
P.O. Box 397
Malta, OH 43758

Marvin Windows
Warroad, MN 56763

Mon-Ray Windows, Inc.
6118 Wayzata Blvd.
Minneapolis, MN 55416

Norton Co.
Sealant Operations
Granville, NY 12832

The Pease Co.
900 Forest Ave.
Hamilton, OH 45012

Ponderosa Pine Woodwork
Yeon Bldg.
Portland, OR 97204

R.O.W. Window Sales Co.
1365 Academy Ave.
Ferndale, MI 48220

Remington Aluminum
Div. of Evans Prods.
100 Andrews Rd.
Hicksville, NY 11801

Reynolds Metals Co.
325 West Touhy Ave.
Park Ridge, IL 60068

Rimco Div., Rodman Industries
P.O. Box 97
Rock Island, IL 61201

Rolscreen Co.
100 Main St.
Pella, IA 50219

Rusco Ind. Inc. Rusco Division
Box 124
Cochronton, PA 16314

Season All Ind., Inc.
Indiana, PA 15701

Geo. C. Vaughan & Sons
223 S. Frio St.
San Antonio, TX 78207

Winter Seal of Flint, Inc.
209 Elm St.
Holly, MI 48442

Zegers, Inc.
16727 Chicago Ave.
Lansing, IL 60438

INDEX